Complimentary Copy

Social Security

A NON-BIBLICAL PERSPECTIVE

Mark Shemtob

**A CONCISE & OBJECTIVE REVIEW
OF THE PROGRAM'S
PAST, PRESENT & FUTURE**

XAVIER PUBLISHING

ISBN   0-9767240-0-6

Published in the United States by

Xavier Publishing,
Morristown,
New Jersey

ACKNOWLEDGMENTS

Thanks to my wife Jane of almost 25 years for her enthusiastic assistance, encouragement, and support. I hope never to stop bewildering her with my eclectic array of projects.

Thanks to my friends and family who took the time to read over my work and offer constructive ideas.

Thanks to the various professionals at RJ Communications who helped to bring the book to press in record time.

Thanks to Sue Nussbaum, for her editorial services that helped transform my original draft of ideas and run on sentences into a comprehensible work.

Finally thanks to those special interest groups, biased media, and tunnel vision politicians for giving me the reason to undertake this project.

CONTENTS

PREFACE

Why do we need another Social Security book? You most likely have had exposure to *more* about the Social Security debate this year than you thought was necessary. The premise of this book is that even though you have heard and read a great deal about the subject, you may still be confused about many of the key issues and questions surrounding the debate. Worse yet, the accuracy of the information you rely on to formulate your opinion may be questionable. Here is a little about this book to help you determine if it would be of value in assisting you to understand the current Social Security program and options for the future.

The book is thin: This, you will notice, is not a thick book. In my efforts to engage the services of a literary agent for representation to potential publishers, the same comment came up several times. *The book was too short.* I purposely made it brief, based on my personal experience. I tend to finish reading non-fiction books if they are not too long. Assuming that this was probably not peculiar to me alone, shorter seemed the logical choice. However, the book does not omit any discussions of topics that I felt were crucial to understanding this debate along with the implications of proposed changes to the Social Security program.

The book is easy to read. This book is not intended for specialists, such as actuaries, economists, public policy consultants or other experts in the field. It is written for the general public who have very legitimate concerns about this topic of national debate, but do not want nor have the time to study the issues in depth. They need more than an endless array of short but often confusing and contradictory reports and articles. The book has no graphs, nor are there discussions regarding productivity trends, the GDP, the GNP, or any other complicated economic concepts. There are some tables in the Appendix that I think are helpful in understanding some trends of significance but they are not critical to the reading or understanding of the book. The reader should require no reference aids either. I have also avoided the use of footnotes, but do reference my sources after the conclusion of the book.

The book is honest: I have not written this book from the viewpoint of a lobbyist or any special interest group. My agenda is simply to educate. I present the issues from both sides, without prejudice. There are enough positions in print already that employ data in a selective manner for drawing the reader to a pre-determined position.

The book is objective: We have all heard from some very smart people that the Social Security system is going broke. We have heard from some other very smart people that this same system is *not* going broke. Since we do not know what *broke* is, it is hard to determine which smart people are smarter. We have also heard many "experts" claim that private accounts are *better* while other "experts" vehemently disagree with that claim. Once again, not knowing who the *experts* are or what *better* means puts us at a disadvantage. My book approaches the relevant issues from all points of view, without declaring broke or not broke, better or worse. There are questions central to the debate that cannot be answered definitively. This book should help you to understand why.

The book includes a little humor: It is not that Social Security reform is a humorous topic. However, a little levity can often make a book easier to read. I, for one, cannot help but chuckle when considering how different Social Security experts reach very different conclusions using identical data.

I hope that you will feel that the book is worthy of your money and your time. One could hardly expect a book on Social Security to be a best seller. Several literary agents warned me that the American public would not buy books covering issues of public policy. These agents claimed that the public would rather listen to the media, regardless of the fact that it is often biased. I hope that this unique examination of such a very important topic, along with an approach that emphasizes brevity, honesty, objectivity and a bit of humor will make a difference.

INTRODUCTION

I started writing this short book from the point of view of an actuary. Since most people are not familiar with what it is, precisely, that an actuary does, I will provide a brief description. An actuary is a highly skilled professional, trained to evaluate the financial costs associated with future unknown events. Actuaries usually work in the insurance, employee benefits or investment professions. They design and employ the mathematical models used in providing answers to very complicated financial questions that involve risk. An actuarial analysis can provide reasonable but different answers to the same financial problem. This is entirely possible because uncertain future events have not yet happened. An actuarial model incorporates *assumptions* regarding the probability of a future event occurring. These assumptions do not just include *if it will happen* but *when it will happen* and the financial implications associated with the event. Different sets of assumptions inevitably, lead to different conclusions. An actuary should always disclose when providing an actuarial analysis the assumptions and methods used in the determination of the results presented. This book is *not* an actuarial analysis of the Social Security system or any proposals for change.

In my particular case, my expertise as an actuary is associated with retirement programs. I provide consulting services to different employers in the establishment of new retirement programs. I also assist employers currently maintaining plans by analyzing their current programs. I help my clients to determine the type and design of the retirement program that best suits their goals or whether their existing program might benefit from modification. Part of this process often includes the establishment of a funding approach to help insure the delivery of benefits. A retirement program that is not properly funded poses serious financial, legal, and participant relation problems.

In addition to my work as a retirement plan consultant, I teach a course in the Finance Department at Rutgers University. The course looks at our nation's varying retirement programs. It covers the design, funding, and taxation elements of a wide range of different types of plans. These include programs for individuals, for small businesses and for those sponsored by large companies. The course also covers, in some detail, an analysis of our nation's Social Security program. I start this topic by trying to determine what the students actually know about the program. I first inquire as to how many have ever paid Social Security taxes. The majority acknowledge that they have. Some students are less certain until we clarify that the annoying deduction on their pay stub, called FICA, is their Social Security tax deduction. We then discuss detailed issues regarding the Social Security taxes paid and the benefits provided by the program. These Finance majors, many of whom are capable of discussing price elasticity and labor force to productivity ratios, offer that they know very little about the program. However, they are aware that the taxes they pay fund benefits for current retired seniors. Their lack of knowledge is not surprising, since 21 year olds hardly find this topic relevant to their lives. Once the semester is over, many of the students report that Social Security was their favorite topic covered by the course.

Many of them indicated, without any solicitation, that they expected to receive modest or no benefits from the program upon *their* retirement. It is their understanding that the program is heading toward bankruptcy and that drastic action is required to save it. When asked to share their sources for this information, I was dismayed to learn that their primary source was their parents. Here is the largest government sponsored social insurance program in the world affecting nearly every American citizen in a meaningful way. These bright and well-educated students know little about the program other than what their parents share with them. The essence of what their parents communicate is that the program is in crisis. I had hoped, with the emphasis placed on this topic by the media, the President's push for reform, the bombardment of newspaper articles and editorials, the daily television coverage, and the many books on this subject that these parents might have communicated a more comprehensive and insightful position to their children.

This experience led me to start studying the program in even greater depth. I felt that my professional experience would be of great assistance in understanding many of the more complicated and technical issues. I studied the history of the program to date, with an emphasis not only on the economic and actuarial issues but on the social issues as well. I attended conferences and heard private sector experts and government leaders speak on the subject and their visions for change. I attended my local town hall meeting to learn not only my fellow citizens' positions but also the basis for their opinions. I read and listened critically to all the media coverage that I came across. It then became obvious why my students' parents reacted with such a simplistic assessment: They were confused. I then started writing about this topic to share with friends, family, and the media in the hope of helping others to appreciate the relevant issues in a more balanced light.

Is there a Social Security financial crisis? Will private Social Security accounts provide for more enhanced benefits? Has the government misused our Social Security taxes? Ever since these and other related questions have been the focus of the country's attention, the media, politicians and special interest groups have been providing the public with a dizzying array of answers. The answers provided to date, have done little to help a somewhat befuddled public to understand the issues and arrive at committed personal positions. Some, who have been able to develop firm opinions, may be relying on biased information.

The debate over Social Security reform is not new but has only hit its stride recently, because the President has pushed it to the top of his domestic policy agenda. With the emphasis in the private sector of adopting retirement plans with account balances (defined contribution plans) compared to plans providing fixed benefits (defined benefit plans); it was inevitable that we would see discussions about similarly transforming our national retirement program.

Therefore, we come down to the question of whether or not we really need another book about Social Security. Upon reviewing several books on the subject, here is what I discovered. Among the most popular books is one entitled *A Complete Idiot's Guide to Social Security*. I was encouraged upon this discovery, assuming that the market for Social Security books for non-idiots was still wide open. I feel this is a good target market. I located some additional books on the subject. One with the title *Social Security, the Phony Crisis,* and the other *The Looting of Social Security: How the Government is Draining America's Retirement Account.* These titles suggested, to my surprise, that we have more than one Social Security program. A reader would need to first determine, which Social Security program he or she wished to explore. This would be confusing since most of us are under the impression that there is only one Social Security program. Many of the other books I came across assist individuals in applying for their Social Security benefits. One of the more interesting books provides advice on how to qualify for Social Security disability benefits if you are not *actually disabled*. Finally, there were some very scholarly books full of very detailed information about the program. They, however, tended to be very large, often over 400 pages. Some had graphs with intersecting curved lines in different colors that was suppose to tell us something for which our language has no words. Those books were definitely not for idiots. The conclusion I came to, after my review of these more popular books, was that a Social Security book that was short, objective, graph free, did not teach non-disabled people how to qualify for disability benefits, and that was not written for idiots might be of value.

As an instructor and retirement plan consultant, I get enormous pride and satisfaction from teaching and consulting. I am not inclined to tell my students what to think about a particular topic or my clients how to proceed with their specific projects. It is my opinion that the majority of books, newspaper articles, television programs, and political speeches on the Social Security debate have not adequately educated the public. The thrust of what we are hearing is negative rhetoric on proposals for change as well as the consequences of inaction. Much of the public has heard so many contradictory claims with regard to "the Social Security crisis" that they are not sure what action they want the government to take. They will most likely end up relying on our leaders to fix the problem if it is broken, or leave it alone if it is not. That is, if they trust the government enough to act in their best interests.

I have established a couple of goals that I hope my book will accomplish. It is my intention to educate the reader and, to that end, the reader will find the writing clear and under-standable. I have made every effort to avoid any technical issues that are not necessary; however, there are certain complicated topics that would compromise an important point if omitted. In these cases, I have made an extra effort to provide sufficient explanation to minimize confusion. I hope that the reader, upon completing this book, will have the following reactions:

- This is a more complicated issue then we have been led to believe by those either supporting or opposing reform.
- There are valid positions advanced by propo-nents on both sides of the debate.
- I now understand the media's reports on the issues and can distinguish facts from positions.

If after you read this book, you still have an inflexible position as to what should happen with the Social Security program, in addition to not being able to understand other points of view, you may have missed the point, or I may not have done a very good job of explaining it. If, after reading this book, the book has enabled you to solidify a particular position, but you can appreciate that different points of view do deserve consideration, my goal will have been accom-plished. If, however, after you read this book you are not sure what should happen, and you are motivated to ask diffi-cult but direct questions of those who will dictate the outcome, that will be a home run.

Before we move on to the actual Social Security discus-sion there are a couple of additional points that I wish to make. Let me start with the title of the book. In my busi-ness, and I'm sure in many other highly technical profes-sions, when a book is published that the professional community learns to rely on as the definitive source for detailed accurate information, it is referred to as *the Bible.* My book is clearly not *the Bible* on Social Security. It would need to be more than 10 times its current length and be loaded with so much detail as to make it extremely uninviting for the non-expert to read. When many of us think about the Bible, we consider a book full of values and morality that instructs us as to what is right and just. That is certainly not the point of this book. My goal is to teach, not to preach, except for just a little at the very end. So why did I use Biblical references? I felt it would make my book stand out from the competition on the bookshelves as well as help to keep the reader's interest.

The other point I wish to address concerns the issue of objectivity. No matter how the book attempts to be objective, the decisions as to what to include in the book were highly subjective. I could not figure out a way around this paradox, without getting back to the problems of length and detail that I felt were too important to compromise. I did have many of my friends with differing points of view read my drafts and I used their comments to fine tune the finished product, based on their observations as to objectivity. I hope that you will find this book to be fair.

The book purposely does not include any specific proposal for reform. There are many of those out there, new ones added, and old ones evolving. You can find them easily on the Internet. After reading this book, you should better understand the substance of each proposal. I do discuss the specific *components* of some proposals since it would be impossible to evaluate changes without the necessary background on what such changes would mean. The book also avoids addressing the actions taken by other nations in the transformations of their national retirement programs. Though this is a very interesting topic to explore, it should have no bearing on what path we follow here. Each nation comes to the issues of change from different pasts as well as with different goals. In addition, it is not surprising that there is a lot of controversy as to the success or failure of some of the programs adopted elsewhere.

Finally, no information about surveys or polls is included. There are many out there; they are constantly changing and, they are often unreliable, since special interest groups fund many of them.

This book does not have a specific target audience. It should be of value to anyone who wants to learn more about the debate from an objective point of view. If you have a child who is already paying Social Security taxes, or that FICA thing, you may wish to encourage him or her to read this book. Their interests are a crucial part of the issues debated; some might say the only part that truly matters. I hope you will enjoy my attempt at humor along the way and agree that I have not discriminated in favor of any one position when using it.

One

GENESIS

O ut of the chaos brought about by the 1929 stock market crash and the ensuing Great Depression, the New Deal was born. This enormous government program that President Roosevelt delivered to the American people set the course for an expansion of the government's responsibility to its citizens. The hallmark of the New Deal was the Social Security program, which, for millions of Americans, has been no less than a great deal, although according to many proponents of significant Social Security reform, may turn out for future generations to be a *raw* deal.

The program became law in 1935 in the hope of filling a crucial economic and social need. Insurance was necessary to protect millions of Americans against the greatest of all financial risks. If you guessed death, you are wrong. In fact, the larger risk was *not* dying. Back then, company pension plans and personal savings were about as common as eight track tapes are today. A system needed to be devised that would allow seniors to collect pensions but without placing a significant financial burden on the wage earners. If this could be accomplished the financial risks of old age could be diminished. So the Social Security program was established. Though taxes started in 1937, it would take some time to accumulate funds to pay benefits. The first pension was not paid until 1940. The program originally provided for only old age benefits. In later years, the program was modified to provide protection against what we consider the more traditional risks of death and disability

This program was financially feasible thanks to two important elements. First, the ratio of the number of workers to the number of retirees was very large. Back in 1945, five years after the first benefit payments, there were 42 workers for each retiree. At that time, the *maximum* Social Security taxes paid by any one worker was $60 per year. Most workers were subject to less than $60 per year in taxes. To appreciate how much 1945 money is worth in today's dollars we should adjust the $60 to reflect changes in the cost of living. The most common measure used is the Consumer Price Index. By adjusting, the $60 from 1945 to the present time yields approximately $630 in today's dollars. I do not think any of us would balk today if the maximum Social Security taxes were $630 per year. It should be apparent, based on the worker to retiree ratio that substantial benefits were available to the retirees with only a small sacrifice by current wage earners. The program was acceptable to the workers who were paying for retiree's benefits because the taxes were not a large burden. They also could look forward to *their own* old age benefits that younger generations would provide.

The second element that helped to make the program workable was life expectancies. The life expectancy at *birth* for a male at the time the program was established was less than 65 years. Based on this life expectancy, it was possible that many males could actually pay into the program but receive no benefits or small benefits. More importantly, there was not significant expectation of pensioners receiving decades' worth of benefits by living late into their eighties.

We need to remember that the system was designed, based on the needs of our nation at that time and the options available. We will see, as we go along, that among the criticisms of the program is that it no longer accurately reflects many of the current social aspects of our population today. Even though Social Security has evolved through the decades, it has retained its basic character and this character is outdated, according to both critics and even some supporters, in several ways.

We will now turn to a brief summary of the program's current benefits. Many of these benefits were not part of the original program. I have omitted many details that I feel are not needed to appreciate the debate we are facing today. One can obtain detailed information regarding benefits from the Social Security Administration or one of the many books available. When I go into detail that causes your head to hurt, please try to stay with me, there is a good reason why I am subjecting you to it. For those of you who are already familiar with the benefit provisions of the program, I apologize for putting you through this, but read them anyway. There is always the chance that you may pick up a new piece of information.

Coverage: Not all U.S. wage earners are covered by the program. The program does cover in excess of 90% of our nation's workers with reported taxable wages. Local and state governments have the option to elect *not* to be part of the program, as can clergy on religious grounds. Some proposals for change would require all future state and local government workers to participate. There are a couple of additional categories of exclusions, not requiring specific mention. To be eligible for any benefits one must generally have had at least 40 quarters of wages subject to Social Security taxes, though there are some exceptions to the 40-quarter requirement.

Old Age Benefits: This is the original and most common benefit paid by the program. It is a monthly benefit, payable for the life of the worker. There is an annual adjustment made to reflect increases in the Consumer Price Index. The benefits usually commence at Social Security retirement normal age which is either 65 (if born prior to 1938) or 67 (if born after 1959). If you were born from 1938 through 1959, you have a normal retirement age which is between 65 and 67.

There is an option for benefits to commence before the normal retirement age, as early as age 62. The election to take an earlier commencement of benefits requires a reduction in the benefit amount. Individuals with different normal retirement ages because of different years of birth will have a different reduction apply at the same early retirement age. An earnings test could reduce the benefit payable to individuals who continue to work, but who wish to start collecting early benefits, prior to the normal retirement age. For those individuals who elect to defer payment of their benefits to an age beyond normal retirement age, an increased benefit amount is payable. The level of the increased benefit depends on the age at commencement and the individual's normal Social Security retirement age. Beyond age 70, however, there is no increase.

The calculation of the benefit to be paid is based upon an average of Social Security taxable wages over a 35-year period. The use of 35 years will come into the discussion later when compared with a private account scenario where all years of covered wages would count in the determination of the benefits. Under the current program individuals with less than 35 years of Social Security taxable wages, have $0 used in determining the average for each year less than 35 without covered wages. If the worker has more than 35 years of covered wages, the 35 years that provide the greatest average is used.

When determining the average wages, there is an initial step referred to as *indexing*. This step takes *each* year's *actual* wages and adjusts it for the increase in the nation's average wages from the year earned to age 60. Therefore, a worker's wages are valued according to their worth nearer the time of *retirement*, not at the time they are earned. For example, assume a worker earned $20,000 in 1980. Further, assume that the average wages earned by a U.S. worker is twice as high at age 60 for this worker than they were in 1980. In place of the $20,000, actually earned, $40,000 would be the number used to calculate the worker's average earnings. The manner of indexing wages is addressed later in the book since there are proposals that would significantly modify the current method. These indexed average earnings are used in the formula that determines the primary benefit payable at normal retirement age. This benefit may then be further adjusted depending on whether the worker elected an early or a late (deferred) retirement. The actual formula used to determine the primary benefit is designed to significantly favor the benefits of lower wage earners relative to higher wage earners. For example, an individual with average wages of $50,000 will get significantly less than twice the benefit payable to a worker with $25,000 of average wages. This approach is referred to as a progressive formula and will come up repeatedly in the book.

Disability: This feature was added to the program in the 1950s to provide benefits to workers who are forced to cease working prior to eligibility for old age benefits. To be eligible, one must demonstrate an inability to engage in substantial gainful employment expected to last for at least 12 months. Approximately 16% of all current benefit recipients are receiving Social Security *disability* benefits. It is generally considered difficult to qualify for Social Security disability benefits. I suppose this is the reason that the Social Security book on disability qualification assistance that I referred to in the introduction may be popular.

Survivor Benefits: The program provides for benefit payments to eligible beneficiaries of deceased wage earners, old age pensioners, and disability pensioners. The eligible beneficiaries are widows, widowers, dependent children, and dependent grandchildren. There are restrictions on the ages of the children and grandchildren for eligibility. There are also restrictions on marriage periods to prevent deathbed nuptials. There are *no* benefits available for other classes of beneficiaries. This could cause an individual to pay a lifetime of taxes and have no death benefit payable to himself or herself or a beneficiary. This issue has caused serious discontent among some citizens. We will address this later in the book.

Dependent Benefits: The program provides for supplementary payments to eligible dependents of retired wage earners. Eligible dependents are spouses, minor children, and dependent parents. There are overall maximum family benefits to prevent the payment of huge benefits to a single family with many eligible dependents. A spouse's dependent benefit entitlement is 50% of the retirees benefit amount. However, if the spouse qualifies for a Social Security benefit based upon his or her own wage history that exceeds the 50% benefit level, then the benefit payable will *not* be the dependent benefit but the spouse's own retirement benefit. The programs dependent benefit provision can create a situation where a married couple with two wage earners can receive less in benefits than a married couple with a single wage earner and the same total family Social Security wage history. This is another instance of inequity that many believe should be addressed.

Medicare: Medicare is the newest benefit feature under the Social Security program but is *not* part of the current Social Security debate. Medicare provides medical benefits for eligible Social Security retirees but generally not before age 65. The Medicare program is managed separately from the pension program. Even though the current national Social Security debate does not involve Medicare, a separate debate is gathering steam, as it becomes apparent that the financial condition of the Medicare program is far worse than the pension portion. I will make no further references in this book to Medicare inasmuch as it would require its own book. I will only be focusing on the pension portion of the program, referred to as OASDI or Old Age Survivor and Disability Insurance.

Now that I have briefly covered the benefits portion of the program, it is time to tackle the financing elements. Social Security benefits are paid from a trust fund. There are actually two trust funds; one for old age and survivors' benefits and the other for disability benefits. I will, however, discuss them as one fund, as is often done. The Trust Fund(s) receives revenue from three sources. The primary source is the Social Security tax under the Federal Insurance Contribution Act or FICA. FICA taxes also include taxes for Medicare, which I had promised not to mention again. Sorry! The other income sources are federal income taxes paid on Social Security benefits, which started in 1984, and interest paid on the Trust Fund investments. The next chapter will address the Trust Fund investments in detail. FICA has three pieces to it, one piece for old age and survivor insurance, one piece for disability insurance and the last for Medicare (oops, there I go again). The current combined OASDI FICA tax rate is 6.2% payable by the worker and 6.2% payable by the Employer, in other words, equal payments from each. It has been at this level since 1990. Individuals who are self-employed pay the entire 12.4% rate. Most economists take the position that the worker is actually paying the full 12.4% since the employer's share is often classified as a fringe benefit. The conventional thinking is that if there were no Social Security program, each employer would pay their share of the payroll taxes to their employees (presumably to save for retirement) as additional wages. Some may disagree, but they are in the minority. I will, henceforth, refer to the rate as 12.4%. In 1945, the Social Security tax rate was only 2%. This was before the addition of many of the features that are now part of the program.

There is a limit on the amount of wages to which the OASDI rate applies. This limit is referred to as the Social Security Wage Base. That level is currently $90,000 and increases each year by the change in the nation's average wages. The wage base limit in 1945 was $3,000. The combination of the 12.4% rate and the $90,000 limit produces a current total *maximum* contribution of $11,160. Previously I noted that the maximum tax from 1945 indexed to the present time was $630. That figure amounts to nearly an 18-fold increase. What was a very cost effective benefit program has certainly changed over time. Among the many reasons for this increase are the additions of disability, survivor, and dependent benefits, as well as the introduction of early retirement options. As you will discover there are other even more significant reasons.

Before moving on, let us take a moment to address the way in which many believe that Social Security is supposed to fit into the overall retirement picture. It was intended to be one of the three legs of the tripod of retirement security. The other two legs are employer sponsored retirement plans and personal savings. Unfortunately, for too many of our retirees this has not been the case. A very significant percentage of our retirees would now be living well below the poverty level if not for their Social Security checks. Advocates of maintaining the current system point to this fact as proof that we need to keep the current Social Security structure intact. Others claim that it has become the crutch that it was never intended to be, putting an unfair burden on some workers and discouraging others from taking more personal responsibility.

In summary, the program was designed approximately 70 years ago providing for the payment of monthly pensions to wage earners upon retirement at age 65. The program has evolved through the years to include additional benefits. The benefits are based on a progressive formula thus providing enhanced benefits to lower wage earners. The program is primarily financed by a tax on the wages of current workers. The taxable amounts were very modest at the program's inception but have risen dramatically through the years. With that background behind us, let us move on and explore details of the Social Security Trust Fund.

Two

TREE OF KNOWLEDGE

W here do our Social Security taxes actually go? How is the Trust Fund invested? Are these funds segregated and locked away waiting to be used for our retirement?

The taxes we pay go into the Trust Fund, most of which are then used to pay benefits to current retirees. There are, however, more taxes being collected currently then there are benefit payments being made. So what happens to these excess dollars? Before we can answer that question, a short lesson on types of retirement plans and the different funding approaches would be beneficial. This will also be helpful when we discuss the comparison of the current Social Security program with the primary proposals for reform.

Many of us work for companies that sponsor 401(k) plans or other types of defined contribution plans. The plan contributions are deposited into an account to be invested. These plans provide no guaranteed benefits at retirement. We are only entitled to the account balance that represents the sum of all contributions made to the plan on our behalf plus or minus investment earnings or losses. Under these types of plans, all contributions are fully funded into the trust accounts and there are no benefits beyond the account balances. Plan participants are happy with these plans when the plan investments perform well. Many of these plans permit, to a certain extent, that the participants control the investment selection of their accounts.

Some of us may also be covered under a defined benefit plan. Defined benefit plans pay to each plan participant a *fixed* retirement benefit. The benefit is based on a formula that generally reflects years of service with the employer and, in some instances, may also reflect average salary history. The level of benefit paid at retirement is generally not known until the individual actually does retire. The benefits payable (unlike those provided by 401k or other defined contribution plans) are not affected by investment gains or losses. The plan participant is, therefore, not concerned with the plan's investment performance. In many ways, defined benefit plans are very similar to the Social Security program.

Even though the actual benefit under a defined benefit plan may not be known for many years, they are often pre-funded in order to insure that there will be sufficient assets available to pay the retirees, once the benefits are due. To accomplish this, the professional services of an actuary is required to project the expected benefits to be paid and at what dates. This is useful in developing an orderly funding program that helps to insure that sufficient assets are available when each employee retires. This is particularly important if a large number of employees are expected to retire at the same time. The Internal Revenue Service requires that plans sponsored by businesses be pre-funded if they are to qualify for favorable tax treatment. There are defined benefit plans that are not pre-funded but operate on a pay as you go basis. They are either not granted favorable tax treatment, or are sponsored by a public or non-profit organization. Under these plans, enough money needs to be deposited in the plan trust, to keep up with benefit entitlements. This type of funding is referred to as "pay as you go."

Social Security is primarily a "pay as you go" program. There is, however, some advanced funding of future benefit liabilities. From the inception of the program in 1937 through 1956, the Trust Fund had accumulated a $23 billion surplus. That is the difference, on an accumulated basis, between the income collected (payroll taxes and interest on investments) and the expenses (benefit payments and administrative costs). During the next 25 years, the surplus grew to only $25 billion. The projected expenses over the next several years were estimated to exceed the expected income by more than $25 billion. Consequently, the $25 billion surplus would not be sufficient to keep the fund solvent. Action was needed if the program was going to be able to honor its benefit promises. Therefore, in 1981, changes were made to modify the program in order to increase its revenue.

Even more significant changes were made in 1983 to further strengthen the program's finances through a combination of tax increases and benefit reductions. These changes were made in the hope of preventing a solvency problem from reoccurring for many decades. The Social Security actuaries were instructed to do projections of benefits going forward 75 years in order to determine what tax rate would keep the program solvent for that period. It is from those calculations that the current 12.4% rate was established. Because of this increased tax rate (which became fully effective in 1990), a sizable Trust Fund surplus has been accumulating; it now exceeds $1.6 trillion and is still growing.

So where is the $1.6 trillion? The amounts being paid into the Trust Fund are, legally, nothing more than taxes. They are not contributions to a retirement plan that is set aside exclusively for the participants of that plan. Under the provisions of the Social Security law, funds that are not needed to pay current benefits and expenses must be invested in special U.S. Government securities. They cannot be invested in stocks, corporate bonds, foreign bonds, municipal bonds, real estate, precious metals, or any other investment type.

So what are these special U.S. securities where the excess funds are invested? They are loans backed by the full faith and credit of the U.S. government. Some like to refer to them as IOUs since hard assets do not back them. They pay interest to the Social Security Trust Fund. The interest rates vary depending on when the loans were made and currently range between 3.5% and 8.75%. Those with the higher rates will be maturing shortly to be replaced with loans at much lower rates. This is because interest rates are now much lower than they were when the high rate loans were issued. The interest does not actually have to be paid to the Trust Fund because *current* taxes collected exceed *current* benefit payments. The interest is accruing as an additional loan from the government to the Trust Fund. If, on the other hand, the interest were actually paid, it would just create an additional surplus which would then be loaned back to the government.

So what is the government doing with these funds? The federal government, for many years now, has been running budget deficits. The national debt is now nearly $7.8 trillion and growing. The government consistently spends more on programs than it collects in income taxes. The annual surpluses from the Social Security program are being used to fund *non* OASDI Social Security programs including defense, Medicare, education, transportation, and all the other programs we have come to rely on. It should be noted that the annual Social Security surplus is *not* even sufficient to cover the annual budget deficit, thus requiring additional borrowing by the federal government.

If the annual surpluses were not loaned to the government, how would the government pay its expenses? It could raise income taxes, reduce spending, or borrow funds elsewhere. The lawmakers appear not to be inclined to do any of these things, since the first two make us taxpayers unhappy, and the third one makes their inability to balance a budget look even worse than it already does. The use of the Social Security surplus makes the annual budget deficits look smaller than they actually are because the Social Security budget is lumped together with the general budget.

Why must the Social Security surplus be invested in government securities? It is the law, for one thing, and U.S. government securities are deemed the *safest* investments in the world. The U.S. government can always raise taxes to obtain revenue or supposedly borrow elsewhere. The law could be amended which might require the current surplus be repaid to the Trust Fund sooner than anticipated as well as requiring that future surpluses not be available for the government to borrow. The government would then need to raise taxes, cut spending, or borrow money elsewhere to repay the current debt, and to finance future deficits.

How would the money be invested if it were not required that it be loaned to the government? This question is so controversial that many of our leaders use it as the reason for not considering legislation to permit alternative investments. There are however, critics who feel that this is just an excuse to continue to allow these excess funds to be available to the federal government. If the money were invested in a trust that included non-U.S. government securities, the Trustees of the Social Security Administration would need to retain *independent* investment managers. These professionals would need to be responsible solely to the Social Security program participants, which of course mean most of us. The Social Security administration would have to provide specific guidelines as to the types and allocations of investments permitted. This would be necessary to limit risk through diversification. The challenges that this option would present should not be under-appreciated. The process of selecting investment managers and developing investment policy guidelines would be extremely complicated.

In my introduction, I mentioned a couple of books that have been written on the Social Security issue. The one book titled, *The Looting of Social Security, How the Government Is Draining America's Retirement Accounts* is about this topic. I hope you can appreciate that the situation is not quite as severe as the book title might indicate but is something that we should recognize as a potential problem. I have not actually used any material from that book. The federal government certainly intends to repay this debt as required. However, might it not be more prudent for the Trust Fund to have some harder assets in lieu of only government IOUs? When the time comes to repay the Trust Fund, what hardships will we endure in order to meet those obligations? Many would also agree that it might be better for the government, in developing responsible budgets, if it were not permitted to use these funds. Finally, there are those who believe that a well-diversified portfolio of assets would generate a better return for the Trust Fund than the current government securities. This would improve the financial status of the program. Those who oppose this idea, and there are many, correctly point out that there would be more potential investment risk with assets that are not backed by the U.S. government. It is a complicated question devoid of a clear answer. There are *not* many in government who advocate allowing the Trust Fund to invest outside of U.S. government securities. On that note, we move on to discuss the program's financial position.

Three

NUMBERS

E arlier, I referenced a book entitled *Social Security the Phony Crisis.* Among the objectives of that book is to raise suspicion regarding the extent of the well-publicized financial problems that the Social Security program faces. I have not actually used any material from that book. Many experts disclaim the notion of a financial crisis that necessitates a radical overhaul of the current system. Their position is that the actual financial problems the program faces are being exaggerated to convince the public that drastic changes are needed to save Social Security.

We will now explore the issue of the program's finances to evaluate the need for action, as well as the extent of that need. This, as you probably already realize, is a complicated subject. We have read numerous reports and heard many speeches on the extent of the program's financial problems. Large numbers are often cited without an explanation as to what they represent. The numbers presented often differ based upon political agendas. What sense can we make out of this confusion?

However, before we get to that question we need a short tutorial on how we access the financial solvency of a program that is based upon uncertain future events. The first step is to retain the services of someone who can see into the future. Unfortunately, people who claim to possess such a gift are often just *possessed.* We therefore have to rely on economists instead, to make the financial assumptions and other qualified experts to make assumptions regarding demographic trends. Economists are usually far more reliable than clairvoyants but they are generally less entertaining.

There are thousands of assumptions covering the likelihood of future events that are needed to project the program's anticipated income and expenses. For example, if we were to make the assumption that a meteor will hit the earth in the year 2010, wiping us all out, there would be no need for a projection of future income or expenses for the years following 2010, thus eliminating a lot of work, and the need for this book. The next chapter will include a discussion of the applicable assumptions with an emphasis on the more significant ones used in the projections.

Another critical element central to these calculations is the time horizon that we want to consider in the measurement of fiscal solvency. Should we project out 10 years, 25 years, 50 years, 100 years, or perpetuity? The idea of perpetuity seems odd, but in a program that transfers liabilities from one generation to the following, it is not without merit to consider. The problem with projecting too far into the future is that the further we look, the more difficult it is to devise accurate assumptions. Additionally, if we go out beyond 100 years, none of us will likely give a damn since we *should* no longer be collecting benefits. Though ocassionally dead people are not reported to the Social Security administration until long after their demise, thus continuing to receive benefits in the hereafter.

How about those funds that represent the Trust Fund surplus that, as we have discovered, are now being used as loans to the Federal government? Clearly we will require those funds because of the expected onslaught of baby boomer retirements. Is it possible that the government could renege on these loans? One would assume not, however, there always is the possibility that the federal government could be so highly leveraged that the repayment of these funds might create even larger economic problems. One solution would be to cut benefits instead.

The term "guaranteed" is often used in describing the program's benefits. However, are the benefits *truly* guaranteed? Back in the early 1980s, the program was modified to reduce the value of future benefit promises by increasing the normal retirement age for those workers born after 1937. A lawsuit was filed against the government, claiming that workers were being denied benefits guaranteed under the Social Security law. The courts ruled in favor of the government. Therefore, guarantee is not always, what we think it is.

Before we actually look at some real numbers, we should look at some fake numbers to enable you to understand the real numbers. There is one technical concept of importance that requires some explanation. We need to make clear the difference between a *cash flow analysis* and a *present value analysis*. A cash flow basis looks at the flow of all money (contributions, investment earnings, benefits, administrative charges) on a yearly basis. In addition, if there is an asset or liability balance present at the beginning of the year that is also taken into account.

A present value (PV) calculation is more complicated. The purpose of a present value calculation is to quantify, in today's dollars, both projected future income and expenses. This is done by taking into account the relative *time value* of money. For example a payment of $1,000 in a couple of years from now is not equivalent to $1,000 today since you can invest less than $1,000 today and have it increase to $1,000 in a couple of years. We must also consider the *probability* that the projected future income and expenses will actually materialize.

For example, assume that I have promised my teenage son that I will give him $100 in 2 years if he does not receive a speeding ticket during that period. In order to determine the present value of this projected benefit to my son, I first need to make some assumptions. I assume that $100 in 2 years is worth $ 95 today, based on a 2-year C.D. rate I got from my local bank. I also assume, based on my research of the driving records for new male drivers that there is a 25% probability of my son getting a speeding ticket during the first 2 years of having a license. My calculation of the present value of the liability of this benefit is $100 x.95x.75 = $71.25 The .95 reflects the 2 year time value of money and the .75 is the probability of my son avoiding a speeding ticket in the first 2 years. Now, in my son's case it will either cost me $0 if he gets the ticket or $100 if he does not. However, the present value of this expense I am assuming is $71.25. If I had 100 sons to whom I offered this deal, I would expect to pay out approximately 100 x $ 71.25 or $7,125 in *today's* dollars.

In a more complicated scenario, there are multiple projections of expected income (contributions) and expected expenses (benefits and administrative charges). The series of expenses are discounted back to the present time based on the relevant assumptions and the time value of money. Similar calculations are performed with the expected income projections. The total present value of the expenses less the total present value of the income less any current assets is the present value of the unfunded obligation. This represents the value in *today's* dollars of the future benefits for which we have insufficient current or future assets. Future assets being the projected *contribution* income we are expecting to collect.

Below is the simplified example I promised. We will assume a 5-year time horizon and current assets of 100.

Future Expenses and Income:

Year	Expenses	Income
1	50	35
2	55	30
3	60	40
4	60	15
5	45	20

Cash Flow Analysis:

Year	Cash Flow
1	100 - 50 + 35 = 85
2	85 - 55 + 30 = 60
3	60 - 60 + 40 = 40
4	40 - 60 + 15 = (5)
5	(5) - 45 + 20 = (30)

As you can see, the program becomes insolvent in year 4.

Present Value Analysis (based on relevant assumptions)

Year	PV Expenses	PV Income
1	48	30
2	45	22
3	45	28
4	43	8
5	30	5
Total	211	93

The total present value of expenses of 211, less the total present value of income of 93, less the current assets of 100, yields a present value of unfunded obligations of 18.

Both scenarios represent different views of the fiscal problem. The Annual Report of the Social Security Trustees provides calculations using both approaches since they provide different measures. Under a cash flow analysis, we discover *when* we are likely to run out of money. The present value calculation attempts to *quantify* the extent of the value of any unfunded obligation in a single sum, using today's dollars.

Now that the tutorial is behind us, we can look at the numbers provided by the Social Security trustees in their 2004 report. The report provides calculations using three sets of assumptions; a pessimistic set, an optimistic set and an intermediate set. The intermediate set is the one used regularly for policy analysis. The other sets of assumptions are used sparingly sometimes by special interest groups when they attempt to make a point. The assumption is that the Social Security Trust Fund surplus will be repaid by the Federal government as required. Here is a summary of results:

- The Trust Fund is adequately funded for the next 13 years on a cash flow basis. Social Security taxes and income taxes on Social Security benefits will *exceed* benefits and administrative expenses.
- Starting in the year 2018, the Social Security taxes and income taxes on benefits will be less than the Social Security benefits plus administrative expenses. In order to continue to pay full benefits without any program changes, the Federal government will need to start *repaying*

back what has been borrowed, to the Trust Fund.

- In order to restore projected 75 year cash flow solvency to the program, it would be necessary to *immediately* increase the current Social Security tax rate from 12.4% to 14.3 % *or immediately* reduce all current and future benefits by approximately 13%.

- If there are no modifications, the Federal government will have fully repaid the Trust Fund all amounts owed by 2042. The projected Social Security taxes plus income taxes on benefits will be the only income available to pay benefits starting in 2042.This income would only be sufficient to fund 73% of the promised benefits in 2042 and would decrease gradually to provide only 68% of the benefits by 2078. In order to pay the full benefits, the payroll tax rate would need to increase from 12.4% to approximately 16.9% in 2042 with a gradual increase to 18.3% by 2078.

The information above relates to the cash flow solvency issues. If we were to look at a present value determination, it also paints a picture of inadequate funding but from a different perspective. If we consider *only* those workers and retirees who are currently covered under the program, the present value of the unfunded obligation is approximately $11.2 trillion. This means that based on the current program's expected expenses and income we would need $11.2 trillion more dollars in the Trust Fund today to avoid any future benefit reductions or Social Security tax *increases.* This would put the program into actuarial balance, which is the hallmark of a well-funded retirement plan. For a program to be in actuarial balance there is no need for additional current assets since current assets in addition to future income would be sufficient to cover current and future expenses. No one is advocating that we fund this $11.2 trillion dollars currently. Wherever would we find it? This is a number that has been mentioned by politicians, special interest groups and the media. I thought you might want to understand what it actually represents.

I guess we can see why the issue of solvency might confuse the public and that some might hope for the meteor. Here are a couple of conclusions that one can reasonably reach. The program is solvent on a short-term basis. If the government repays its debt to the fund, the program should be solvent on an intermediate term basis. The program is very unlikely to be solvent on a long-term basis. The longer we wait to make adjustments, the more costly they will be to future generations.

Four

SARAH AND METHUSELAH

I f we all had continued to begat, in the same manner as
they did in the Bible, today's Social Security debate may
never have seen the light of day. For the most part, the majority of Americans are following in the footsteps of Sarah and
producing smaller families. Then we have the followers of
Methuselah who according to the Bible lived to 969. There
are currently in excess of 75,000 centenarians in the U.S. It
is anticipated that this amount will double every decade. No
other age group can make that claim. Methuselah would be
proud. The problem is that our Social Security system
depends on the intergenerational funding of benefits. Fewer
children provide for less taxpayers; that is bad. Longevity
means that many people are getting benefits longer; that is
also bad.

So just how bad is this ratio of workers to retirees going
to become? By 2025, the ratio will be 2.3 workers for each
retiree. By 2040, it will be 2 to 1. This is very different from
1945 when the ratio was 42 to 1. It is not surprising that
students learning about Social Security are dumbfounded,
not by the fact that we have smaller families and longer life
expectancies, but that we did not see it coming. Worse yet,
that we choose to ignore it at their expense. So which is it,
stupidity, or greed?

The financing of the program depends upon the ability
of economists and other experts to make predictions about

the future, and the skill of actuaries to build a mathematical model to project the income and the expenses. This is necessary to arrive at either a cash flow analysis, which helps us to determine when we will run out of money, or the present value of unfunded liability, which tells us how much money must drop from the heavens today to bring the plan into actuarial balance. The actuaries, of course, do a splendid job with their actuarial modeling and number crunching. The economists and other predictors of the future have a more challenging job. Here is a brief list of the areas about which they need to develop assumptions.

- Life expectancy rates for workers and retirees by gender
- Fertility rates
- Immigration rates
- Emigration rates
- Disability incidence rates
- Life expectancy rates for disability retirees by gender
- Expected rates of return on trust fund investments
- Expected increases in the consumer price index
- Expected increase in national average earnings
- Expected cost to administer the program
- Expected income taxes to be collected on benefit payments
- Probability of retirees having dependents
- Projected unemployment rates
- Probability of a meteor hitting the earth (not really)

There are certainly others, but you should get the point. As the assumptions go further into the future, it becomes more and more difficult to rely on their accuracy in providing meaningful projections. The accuracy level of a 10-year projection will be very different from one for a 75-year projection.

As discussed in a previous chapter, back in the early 1980s when the system was on the brink of being unable to meet its benefit obligations the primary solution was a gradual Social Security tax rate increase. The Social Security actuaries, based on assumptions selected by the plan trustees, and with the assistance of the economists and other demographic experts, determined that a 12.4% rate would provide for 75-year cash flow solvency. This 12.4% rate was not projected to hold beyond 75 years or the year, 2058. The calculations that the actuaries have provided in the 2004 Social Security report, predict solvency only through 2042 based on the intermediate set of assumptions. Why will the fund run short 16 years ahead of schedule? Remember that the 1983 projections were based on many assumptions, and apparently, those assumptions taken together turned out to be too optimistic. The two main assumptions that caused this to occur were fertility (too few children) and life expectancy rates (people living longer). It is also possible that the program will be solvent beyond 2042, or become insolvent prior to that time. The Congressional Budget Office projects the insolvency date to 2052, only 6 years shy of the 2058 projection. How is that possible? If you answered that this can be accomplished by using different sets of assumptions, then give yourself an **A**. Some assumptions will increase projected income, such as higher interest rates on the Trust Fund investments, or higher fertility and immigration rates. Others will decrease projected expenses such as lower consumer price index increases, or smaller improvements in future mortality rates. Combine these factors and the result will be a longer period of projected solvency. We will not know the date of actual insolvency until it is upon us.

The inability to know just what the future will hold, coupled with the reality that we can project accurately only on a short term basis, makes for a somewhat inexact science and plenty of debate. If you are surprised that our future retirement may be financed, based upon a system that relies on guesses about the future, you need to appreciate that Social Security is primarily a social *insurance* program and not a retirement program. An insurance program is designed to offer protection against financial risks. Our Social Security program offers insurance protection against the risks of living too long, early retirement because of disability, or leaving dependent survivors without adequate funds upon premature death.

All insurance programs employ assumptions about the future. As a simple example, let us consider life insurance. A life insurance company charges premiums to those who select it to provide a death benefit to the insured's beneficiary. In the determination of the premium that the company will charge the policyholder, they must establish a set of assumptions, which include mortality rates, policy lapse rates (occasionally, the policyholder will stop paying premiums and the insurance is no longer in force), investment return rates, and administrative expense amounts. It is possible that the actual incidence of total deaths for all the policyholders could cause the company to incur death claims that exceed the total premiums collected. State governments require that certain safeguards be followed by insurance companies to minimize this risk; however, it is possible (though unlikely) that an insurance company could default on its benefit payment obligations. The basis of insurance is the *effective* management of risk. The Social Security system is deemed to have *less* risk than an insurance company does, since the Federal government, which administers the program, has the power to raise Social Security taxes if required.

There was one assumption, in particular, that I mentioned previously and which warrants repeating. This is the probability that the Federal government will make good on its debt to the Trust Fund. The Social Security administration, in their annual report, assumes that this is a certainty. This is crucial to the projection of full cash flow solvency to the year 2042. Some critics of the program remain skeptical that the government will meet its full obligations and thus anticipate a solvency problem in 2018. This is why we hear some political claims that the crisis will occur in 2018 as opposed to occurring in 2042. Politically, it is difficult to imagine that the government would default, but not knowing what the world will look like then, one cannot be sure. If the surplus were invested in hard assets, this might *not* be an issue.

Under the best-case scenario, that the government *will* pay back the Trust Fund as required, where will these assets come from? The options are higher income taxes, reduced government programs, or borrowing elsewhere. None of these are attractive alternatives. Higher income taxes and reduced government programs are politically risky and extremely unpopular. Borrowing elsewhere is viable based on today's global economy. It is however possible that investing in U.S. securities in 13 years may not be as attractive to investors as it is today. This could lead to increases in interest rates in order to attract funds, thus leading to inflation or other nasty economic fall-out.

Before we move on to some proposals to improve the Social Security financial picture, I want to do a brief recap of what we have already explored. Social Security is a social insurance program that provides protection to the participating wage earners against the risk of disability, death and, most importantly, old age without employment. It is not intended to be the only source of protection, but for many Americans it is, if not the only one, the primary one. The program uses a progressive benefit formula that provides larger proportional benefits based on wages to those perceived to have the greatest need. The program is financed primarily through a payroll tax that was determined in 1983 to be sufficient to keep the program fully solvent, on a cash flow basis, through the year 2058. The program, though not designed to advance fund benefits, has built up a significant surplus in anticipation of a dramatic shift in the ratio of workers to retirees, as the baby boomers retire. These baby boomers, not only did a dismal job in procreating, but also promise to do a great job in sticking around to collect their benefits for many years. The Trust Fund surplus, by law, must be invested with the government and has been used to finance our national debt. The Social Security administration projects that in 2018 there will no longer be annual surpluses of taxes collected over expenses. Starting in the year 2042, the accumulated surplus will be totally exhausted. These projections are contingent on many assumptions and the actual dates of these events could be sooner or later.

Five

REBUILDING THE TEMPLE

H ere is where we start exploring the options available. The first option is to do nothing. There are two groups comprised of politicians and special interest groups who favor this option but for vastly different reasons. One group would like to see the program run its course, crash and disappear from our national landscape. There are very few in this camp and their philosophy is that small government is good government; therefore, the death of this program would be a dream comes true. The other group, which is much larger in number and louder in their rhetoric, also advocates doing nothing at this time, but for a different reason. They take the position that the program will be solvent for many years to come and that any rush to action is premature and politically motivated. What they are hoping is that in the not too distant future the leadership in Washington will change. At that time, they would pursue modifications to Social Security that correspond with their vision.

The majority of those at the center of the controversy, however, believe that action is required sooner than later. Many proposals have been advanced to date. There are however, two different approaches offered to tackle the problem. This chapter will deal with the approach advocated by those who support maintaining the present social insurance *structure* but providing *modifications* to bring it into improved financial solvency. The next chapter will deal with the more radical approach, the one that is being proposed by the President.

The basic premise behind this rebuilding approach is that the current program has thus far been very successful in achieving its purpose. There is an acknowledgment that our nation has evolved economically, socially, and demographically since the program's initial design. However, restoring the long-term fiscal balance to the system should *not* require modifying it beyond recognition. Those who take this point of view believe strongly in the program's importance as a social insurance system and fear the loss of those provisions that provide insurance against those financial risks associated with death, disability, and old age. In addition, they feel that the structure providing for greater relative benefits for the most needy should not be compromised.

The proposals to resolve the fiscal problem work on two different fronts. First are the changes, which would reduce expenses by reducing future benefits. The other relates to the changes that would increase the amount of future income. I will address the different ideas proposed to accomplish each of these goals, along with some relevant commentary for each idea. This is by no means a complete list or a *specific* proposal. It is a survey of the types of ideas that could be considered by Congress in attempting to improve the current system's long-term fiscal solvency.

The overriding consensus is that there should be a group of citizens who will be unaffected by any changes in the program. These are individuals already receiving benefits. In addition, it is generally believed that those who are within a certain time frame of retirement should not have any changes affect the benefits they are expecting to receive. They would probably be subject to any increase in Social Security taxes if applicable. The age that is most often cited is 55.

We will first address those items that would reduce future benefits.

Change in calculation of Primary Insurance Amount:
The formula that is used to calculate the primary benefit amount from average indexed earnings would be restructured to provide reduced benefits. This would affect the benefits for all wage earners. It is likely that the restructuring would provide the greatest reductions to the highest wage earners.

Increases to the normal retirement age:
As previously addressed, this was done before. Such a change, again, may not be easily accepted, if it affects those workers who were aware of the change the first time it was made in 1983. Previously, workers who were 45 years old, or younger, had their retirement ages pushed back. The rational for such a change in retirement ages again, is that life expectancies have increased over the last 22 years. In addition, workers are now healthier in their 60s and are thus better suited to work to an older age. Early retirement would still be available at the same ages as currently permitted, but would result in a larger reduction in the benefit amount. One might argue that if our nation's younger people do not believe they will get much out of the system then they should not object. In order to obtain the greatest financial impact it is best to have this change apply to as old an age as is politically possible.

Use of alternative indexing for initial benefit determination:
Earlier in Benefit Calculation 101, we touched upon the process that is used to calculate a worker's indexed average wages, which is then used to determine the primary benefit amount. Each year's wages are adjusted to reflect the changes in national average wages from the year the wages were earned to age 60. One idea brought forth is the

possibility of calculating the adjustment based, not on national average wage increases, but on the Consumer Price Index increase. This change would result in smaller indexed average wages and thus smaller benefits. The rational for this approach is that Social Security indexing should be for protection against the risks of inflation and that the Consumer Price Index is the proper measure in this regard. This adjustment would have a dramatic effect on benefit levels. If it were ever adopted, it would most likely be done on a phased in basis, to protect those currently nearest to retirement. In addition, there could be some combined use of both indexes in order to preserve the more progressive feature of the program that benefits the lower wage earners.

The following proposals would increase revenue.

Changes in the Social Security wage base: The wage base is currently $90,000 and increases each year, based on national average wage increases. A popular proposal is to increase the current level of the wage base significantly above $90,000. This rationale is twofold. The first being that these wage earners can best afford to bear the cost of the additional funding needed to bring the program into better financial balance. The second rationale is that higher income earners have experienced greater increases in life expectancies than the general population and thus should be expected to pay a larger percentage of the cost associated with their longevity. Approximately 15% of Social Security taxpayers would be impacted by this change. A large increase in the Social Security Wage Base would most likely receive popular support by a good portion of the public, since a majority of the more recent income tax breaks are considered to have favored high-income individuals.

Increases to the Social Security Tax Rate: The rate has been at 12.4% since 1990. A higher tax rate would certainly be the easiest way to significantly increase revenue. It might also be among the least popular approaches, since all Social Security taxpayers would be affected.

Universal coverage; There are approximately 4 million employees working for state and local governments which have opted out of the Social Security program. These governments have adopted alternative programs for their employees. Prior to the 1983 changes federal employees were also excluded from the program. A requirement that all state and local employees be covered by the program would increase revenue. Of course, there would ultimately be an increase in benefit obligations. In the aggregate, however, there should be a net gain to the program in terms of solvency. This is attributable to the fact that few of these employees are very low paid and many are higher paid. Since the system tends to be a less generous provider of benefits relevant to contributions for the higher paid workers, this proposal should improve the program fiscally. In addition, if the program is restructured it would be done so to improve fiscal solvency. This would require that in the aggregate all new covered workers must ultimately receive *less* out of the system in value than they contribute. This is necessary if the goal is to significantly reduce the unfunded liabilities. The employees and the state and local governments may not embrace a requirement that they participate in the Social Security program. They, however, will have a poor argument against being covered inasmuch as the federal workers took the same plunge in the 1980s. Any change of this type should most likely provide that only new employees be covered by the program. Those employees already working for the state or municipality as of the date of such a change would continue to be covered only by the employer's current retirement program. There is some debate about the amount of money this would save the system in the long run, but it would certainly help the cash flow position of the program in the short and intermediate term.

Trust Fund Investments: This is an idea that gets very little serious support other than by a few outspoken individuals. The law now requires that all Trust Fund assets must be invested in Federal government notes at a fixed rate of return that is established at the time the assets are transferred from the Trust Fund to the Federal treasury. Most educated investors would not place all their investments in one type of investment, but would allocate them among several classes of investments, if they wished to increase returns but have some limits on risk. If the Trust Fund could generate investment earnings that exceed the returns paid by the government notes, this would provide additional revenue and thus a savings to the program. On the other hand, with the issue of the government's need for funds to meet the annual federal budget, the concern over market risks, and the further implications of the government becoming involved with investments in private companies, this idea is not likely to see the light of day.

Other Taxes: This is another possibility that has been offered with little attention, due to the general dislike of taxes. Ideas set forth include the reinstatement of some level of the estate tax which is set to expire in a few years, a special temporary income tax, a consumption tax on luxury items, a special income tax levied on high incomes, special corporate taxes, a national sales tax, or whatever other tax one can imagine.

There certainly are other possibilities as to how the current program can be preserved. If this were the path we pursue, the first challenge would be to determine the extent to which we are prepared to strengthen the program's finances. Do we just preserve cash flow for a certain period of time or do we attempt to significantly reduce the large unfunded liability. The next issue would be to determine how this goal should be achieved, that is, what portion should come from benefit reductions, and what portion should be derived from revenue increases. This would then need to be followed by a determination of which demographic groups should experience the greatest brunt of the changes. In all probability, this would be the youngest citizens and the highest wage earners. I did not mention any changes to accomplish the goals of eliminating some inequities that now exist because of shifts in demographics of our country relative to increases in the number of non-traditional families. These too might be considered if they could be accomplished without meaningful additional liabilities and without changing the insurance and progressive nature of the program.

The current Social Security debate that has caused so much controversy *has not* been about how to preserve the current system by strengthening it, fiscally. So what is the debate really about? Welcome to the Promised Land!

Six

THE PROMISED LAND

We just finished exploring how the current program could be fiscally improved and, at the same time, preserve its basic structure. This is the structure of providing insurance through monthly lifetime pensions, payable on account of old age, disability, and death through a progressive benefit formula. According to President Bush, the direction in which we should move is quite different. His vision would provide for the establishment of individual accounts for each wage earner, to be earmarked exclusively for the benefit of that wage earner and his or her beneficiaries. The individual would control the investment under these individual accounts. There would most likely be some limitations on the investment alternatives available, as well as restrictions on the use of funds prior to retirement. Beyond these basic provisions, the different proposals set forth by different parties vary greatly. The next chapter will explore some of those issues in detail.

I will approach the discussion of private accounts by first addressing the advantages of such a program, as outlined by its advocates. I will next address some of the major issues of opposition to a privatized program as set forth by its opponents, along with some responses to these criticisms.

Ownership: In the real estate business, the expression used when determining what gives a home its value is location,

location, location. In the private account debate, it is ownership, ownership, ownership. This is the number one argument made in support of private accounts. The current
program provides the *promise* of a benefit, payable by the
government, upon the occurrence of permanent disability,
attainment of retirement age, or death (provided one has a
qualified beneficiary). This promise is contingent upon the
government not modifying the law to either reduce or eliminate benefits. It was noted, previously, that the government
has done so in the past, when it changed retirement ages. A
private account would represent to the wage earner a *tangible* asset that would be protected from any government deci-
sion to modify the program's benefits.

Equitable: Many support the idea of private accounts for
what is considered the simple equitable nature of such an
approach. There is no insurance element involved and the
taxpayer receives from his or her account the amount
contributed plus any investment earnings on the contributions made. This is similar in concept to a 401k plan or an
IRA.

Limited Beneficiaries: The current Social Security program
has what many consider to be a significant flaw. It is possible,
under the present system, for a worker to pay taxes for a
working lifetime and never receive a penny in benefits from
the program, or have a benefit provided to his or her beneficiary. Under the current program an eligible beneficiary is
limited to a spouse or minor child. Many workers today have
less traditional families and often may have a non-traditional
beneficiary, to whom they would like their benefits left, upon
their death. Remember that the current program is insurance. In the past, the only beneficiaries that were considered as dependents requiring financial assistance were
spouses and minor children. Private accounts would be

treated like any other asset and could be left as an inheritance to whomever one wished, in the case where there was no eligible dependent spouse or child.

Dual Benefit Eligibility Another feature of the current program that is considered inequitable is the dependent benefit, which is available to the spouse of a retiree, who has never worked or has had extremely low lifetime wages. This benefit is equal to 50% of the retiree's benefit. This can have the effect of providing enhanced benefits to couples where there is only one breadwinner and who has paid the same total amount into the system as couples having two breadwinners. Private accounts would overcome this inequality by providing benefits that are directly related to what was actually paid into the program. It is also pointed out that many homes with just one breadwinner have significant additional assets and there is no need for these enhanced benefits.

Use of Trust Fund surplus: As discussed previously, the government has been using the Social Security tax dollars as a loan to fund non-Social Security expenses. This has contributed to an increase in the national debt. Because these amounts are not held in hard assets that are readily available, the issue is raised regarding the ability to meet all promised benefits in the future. The use of private accounts would curtail the current practice of the government using these funds, since they would not automatically be invested in government notes.

Permanent Fiscal Solvency: Under the current Social Security program, we can never be assured of attaining permanent fiscal solvency. This is the case because the program is a defined benefit plan that relies on actuaries, economists and other experts to estimate future income and expenses. If their estimates are off, this could lead to having insufficient funds to pay benefits in the future. On the other hand, private accounts provide no *fixed* future benefit, only the value of the account. If the nation decides that permanent fiscal solvency is a priority, this could be achieved by ultimately transitioning to a program only comprised of private accounts, since such accounts do not provide fixed lifetime benefits.

Enhanced Investment Returns: Advocates of private accounts insist it would be beneficial to allow investments in private investment markets, which historically have generated greater rates of return than government securities, under the current program. This should translate into bigger retirement accounts at the same cost.

Before addressing the areas of major concern with a privitization approach and the responses put forth by its advocates, we should take a moment to point out the fundamental philosophical difference between the current program and a program of private accounts. The current program is designed as an *insurance* program providing lifetime retirement, disability, and death benefits. A private account approach is a *savings* program, earmarked primarily for retirement, but which carries with it ownership rights. Insurance and savings programs are designed to provide for needs that are not identical. Many taxpayers do not understand that the current program is insurance, but consider it a retirement plan. Therefore, before comparing the two, we need to be reminded that we are comparing apples and oranges.

Let us now look at the principal objections put forth by the private account opposition along with some responses by their advocates. Those who do not oppose privatization outright, but who have legitimate concerns that need to be addressed, also share some of these concerns.

Won't the transition to private accounts be too expensive? The current program uses taxes paid by those working to fund the benefits of current retirees. The use of private accounts will entail the diversion of some of the Social Security taxes to private accounts. Since the same dollar cannot go to two places at the same time, (except in Washington) money used to fund private accounts cannot be used to pay current retiree benefits. The Social Security program is currently running at a surplus, as discussed previously, but at some point this will no longer be the case. In addition, even though there is currently a surplus, the federal government is spending the surplus on non-Social Security expenses, as quickly as it is being collected. So how can we finance such a transition?

The proponents of privatization acknowledge that is very real concern; however, the current program's financial issues are not the result of a proposed change to privatized accounts. Their argument is that there would be no unfunded liability if the program consisted of only private accounts. They also note that privatization may be the only true way to bring permanent solvency to the program. The financial problem exists today regardless of the privatization issue. This should *not* be used as a reason to reject the transformation of Social Security into a more modern program. Some proponents see private accounts as a mechanism to help reduce the *future* liabilities of the current program. They claim that using private markets for the individual accounts will generate larger returns and thus possibly allow the benefits from the traditional program to be reduced for future retirees. More realistic proponents of private accounts do not rule out increases in taxes to fund this transition.

Will low-income workers suffer? Let us start by reiterating that the current program is designed to provide progressive benefits by a formula that weighs benefits toward the lower average wage earners. *Pure* private accounts would *not* provide such a feature.

Proponents of private accounts claim that most low wage earners will *not* be negatively impacted. The arguments set forth are as follows: Traditional Social Security benefits are based on 35 years of wage history. Lower wage earners often start working earlier than higher wage earners due to less higher education and earlier entry into the workforce. They often have more years of wages, exceeding 35, than do higher wage earners. The effect is to reduce the progressive nature of the formula, since the lower wage earners with more than 35 years of service receive back no benefits based on this longer working lifetime. Lower wage earners also tend to have shorter life expectancies, on average, than higher wage earners. Therefore they lose out on the longevity of benefits compared to the higher wage earners.

Is the public knowledgeable enough to be able to make wise long-term investment decisions with their private accounts? This is critical, since the benefits paid from the individual accounts will directly relate to the investment selections made and poor choices could lead to inadequate retirement benefits.

Proponents of private accounts point out that many workers now have experience investing in 401k plans and IRAs where they have received investment education and have been required to make their own investment decisions. This aside, most plans for privatization would have restrictions on the investments available as well as default elections for those not wishing to make their own choice. This issue will be covered in detail in the next chapter.

It is too risky to give up the benefits of guaranteed pensions for benefits subject to market risk. There is no direct investment risk to workers associated with the *current* program. The investment risks associated with private accounts are far more tangible.

Private account proponents make the point that the current program is not totally risk free, since it is subject to the political risk that the government can change benefits by legislative actions. They also point out that private accounts can be structured in a way to limit the risk and yet enhance returns over a portfolio of only government securities. This will be addressed in detail in the next chapter.

What happens if the stock market collapses, right before retirement? You do not have to be too old to have recently experienced the unpleasant phenomenon of having your 401k go to a 201k go to a 101k. Few of us managed to escape the effects of the stock markets meteoric declines, just five or so years ago. Now imagine that you are 65, you did not have a 401k account, employer pension, or any other meaningful personal savings. Your Social Security account is in a stock fund. You get the picture.

Many supporters of private accounts are very aware of this concern and respond as follows: There will need to be some reasonable restrictions on the investments options available that would prevent an individual, nearing retirement age, from having too high a concentration of their account in the stock market. This will also be addressed in the next chapter. Even so, a few proponents acknowledge that it may be necessary to have a safety net built into the system to protect workers from this danger.

Will the financial markets be able to absorb all of this additional capital? If everyone decided (assuming they could) to invest in individual stocks, there would clearly be some serious bubbles created that would eventually burst.

Most supporters of privatized accounts stress that the investment approach must be such that it prevents the creation of such bubbles. They claim that this can best be accomplished by using a very large spectrum of investment classes and by using a very gradual transition into private markets. There is also the position held by some, but not all economists, that this additional capital could help companies to grow and strengthen the U.S. and possibly even the world economy.

Won't a private account system leave those with disability, the dependents of those who die prematurely and those who outlive their accounts financially distressed? Since the private account would be the basis of the benefits, a wage earner in the work force for a short period of time may not have accumulated a sufficient account balance upon early disability or death. In addition, there certainly will be pensioners who will far outlive their life expectancies and their accounts. The current program provides subsidized benefits for such individuals. Since individual accounts are *not* an insurance program, these individuals would be at risk.

It is unlikely that privatized accounts will see the light of day without a satisfactory solution to this problem. The more realistic supporters of Social Security privatization believe that the government must provide some mechanism for insurance to cover these situations.

Won't the bureaucracy of individual accounts be expensive? As an example, assume a worker earns $25,000 per year and the percentage going to a private account is 4 % of wages. This would amount to $1,000 per year. If the worker is paid weekly, this amounts to less than $20 per week. Let us assume it is split among four investment choices. This amounts to $5 per transaction. If that money had to find its way into an individual account each week, the administrative expense could be prohibitive.

This is one of the reasons why private accounts would need to have limited options as well as significant lead-time before implementation. Opponents to private accounts are correct that the administrative burden could be large. However, some concede that, with time, a system could be developed that would bring the administrative costs down to a reasonable level. This would require that limitations and restrictions be placed on the accounts.

There are, undoubtedly, other advantages and disadvantages to a privatized program. My purpose is to examine the key areas in enough detail to frame the debate, in a manner that can open your eyes to the differences between the current system and a system which incorporates private accounts. This is as good a time as any to try to provide a comparison of the two program philosophies that are *not* easily comparable.

In order to try and compare the two programs, we need to start in a similar place. Let us first assume that the issue of unfunded liability does *not* exist under the current program or, more simply, that we are starting a new program today. We will consider two different options. The first one has the current benefit structure with a payroll tax, *sufficient* to fund all anticipated benefits into perpetuity. We will further assume that the economists and our other fortune tellers will be perfect in their predictions of the future so that there will never be any need to change the tax rates or benefit levels.

The other alternative will be a pure privatized account program with identical tax rates (contributions) to the current program, where the amount of benefits payable are *fully* based on the account balances. We will further assume that the total aggregate investment returns and administrative expenses under the *private* account program are identical, in the aggregate, to the *current* program's trust fund government investments and expenses. It therefore must follow that the total benefits available under each program will also be identical, since total benefits must equal total contributions plus total investment earnings less total administrative expenses.

Of course there will be those who, under the current program, fare better relative to the private account program and those who will not. Some of the recipients who would be favored under the *current program* are those who live well beyond their life expectancies, workers with low lifetime wages, those who receive early disability benefits and retirees with many qualified dependents. Some of the recipients who would fare better under a *privatized program* would be participants who die prematurely without an eligible beneficiary, those without covered dependents, workers with higher lifetime wages, and those who make it to retirement but die before receiving many years of benefits.

What would be the effect of using private markets? If private markets were made available only under the private account program and the aggregate investment returns exceeded that earned under government only investments, the total benefits in the aggregate would increase under the private program. There still, however, would be some individuals who would do better under the current fixed benefit program with a lower rate of return than under a private account program with a higher rate of return. It would be a function of the following factors: the individual's wage levels, the actual difference in the rates of return in the private accounts over the government securities in the current program, the number of covered dependents, a spouse's income level where applicable, the incidence of disability, actual longevity, and other additional factors over which we have no control.

What Social Security privatization is essentially about is a reallocation of benefits in a manner that will produce a system without subsidies or guarantees. Many citizens might consider this more equitable, since the worker and his or her heirs would receive from the program the amount actually contributed, *plus* net investment earnings. If anyone tells you that you will definitely fare better under one approach over the other, he or she has a crystal ball, is delusional, or has a set agenda in place.

Seven

THE COVENANT

L et us assume that the American public buys into the President's vision for Social Security private accounts. Our elected officials will then be faced with the difficult job of creating the law that would initiate this immense restructuring of the program. Agreeing on the nuts and bolts of such changes and how and when to implement them would be a huge undertaking. Adding private accounts to Social Security would most likely be just a part of an overall program restructuring. Following are some of the key issues that would need to be included in the development of a Social Security private account program.

Who would be affected by change? There is no debate that those already receiving benefits will continue to be covered under the current program without any modifications. It is also likely that the future increases for these individuals on account of Consumer Price Index changes would be unaffected. It is most probable that there would be a group of *near term* retirees who would continue to be covered exclusively under the current program. Age 55 is the most common cutoff age but not the only age cited. What is not so clear is whether this group would escape *all* changes that might be part of any comprehensive reform to the program. If, for example, the wage base limit was increased, it is likely that this group would be subject to that change.

Would the private account option be voluntary or mandatory? Must all eligible workers participate in private accounts or will there be an option to remain exclusively within the current program of social insurance? What changes might be made to the current social insurance program and how will that impact any options? How will each worker determine which option is in his or her best interest? Who will provide this education? It is likely that those with the greatest dependency on the Social Security program will be the least well equipped to make an informed decision. It is for these reasons that offering a choice of programs might not be the most practical option though it might be the most politically attractive in concept.

When would the private account feature become effective? It will be difficult to quickly implement any massive changes to Social Security. The President's early comments under his "proposal" were that 2009 could be the initial year for private accounts. The mechanics of having Social Security taxes directed into individual accounts for over 150 million workers is not in place. The Federal government does not currently obtain the record of the annual Social Security taxes paid by individuals, until the following year. If applicable, any choices given to workers will necessitate providing ample time for them to study the options available, before they can be expected to make informed decisions. It is clear, based on the current political climate and the many complications involved with any reform, that it would be quite a while before any proposals could be expected to make it into law.

What portion of the Social Security taxes would go towards private accounts? If private accounts did become law, either as an option or on a required basis, what portion of our payroll taxes should be diverted into these accounts?

Would it be fixed or flexible, based upon age, or subject to the election of the taxpayer? Would these funds come from a tax above the 12.4% rate, as some lawmakers have proposed, in order to make the transition less financially difficult? Clearly, there is a limit on what percentage of the current taxes could go toward private accounts, when considering the need to continue to pay current benefits. This will depend not only on the cash flow projections of the Trust Fund but on whether the Federal government is willing to and able to pay back the accumulated Trust Fund surplus, sooner than is currently scheduled. The government's dependency on future annual surpluses over the next 13 years must also be taken into consideration. Without these surpluses, the Federal government will have larger deficits than currently projected. From where will the Federal government get the funds for these more rapidly than expected repayments? Will it be from income tax increases, spending cuts, or borrowing elsewhere?

Will there be any restrictions on the investment options available under private accounts? Opponents of private accounts are claiming that the investment community is quietly licking their chops in anticipation of the trillions of dollars that will be coming their way, should private accounts become law. These opponents warn that the private investment community will take unfair advantage of investors by directing them into holdings that are speculative and self-serving. Several mutual fund companies and investment organizations have recently been implicated in activities that have violated SEC rules, and have been fined for these violations. This clearly has not endeared the private investment community to the public nor to the government regulators.

The ENRON scandal also merits some attention. I heard one opponent to Social Security privatization refer to private accounts as the *Enroning* of Social Security. There has clearly been unconscionable behavior by chief executives of other major corporations that have caused innocent stockholders to lose billions of dollars. Enron is only the poster child. As a result of these scandals a law was passed, *the Sarbanes Oxley Act of 2002* that is intended to help curb the kind of corporate abuses we have recently witnessed. Since the law is relatively new, its effectiveness in protecting shareholders is hard to ascertain.

Even if we assume that the scandals are behind us and that the investment community will not try to profit by marketing inappropriate investments, there are still legitimate concerns about investing in stocks. The motives of some public companies' executives appear to be more focused on short-term results, as opposed to long-term potentials. This has been brought about by some unreasonable expectations that Wall Street has put on these companies to constantly report improved profits in order to increase stock prices.

Some of the proponents of individual accounts desire minimal restrictions placed on options, citing the importance of free choice. However, it is generally acknowledged that any privatization program, that would stand a chance of getting through Congress, will require some serious restrictions in order to satisfy those who raise reasonable objections. If it is perceived that the investment community is destined to score big on privatization, or that an individual's future retirement security could be tied up too heavily in a single or in a just a few stocks, the opposition to privatization would be insurmountable.

Just to give an example of how stock prices can be volatile beyond legitimate business reasons, I reviewed ten of the largest U.S. companies and analyzed their 52-week range in stock prices. I picked only companies that a conservative stock investor would be comfortable including in his or her portfolio:

- American Express
- Citibank
- General Motors
- IBM
- Johnson & Johnson
- Coca Cola
- Exxon
- Wal Mart
- General Electric
- Proctor & Gamble

The average fluctuation in share price over the last 52-week period for these 10 stocks was 30%. Is it reasonable that these stocks could have changed so much in value in only a 52 week period? Did Johnson & Johnson have that much fluctuation in Q-tips sales or Proctor & Gamble with their toilet paper sales to justify such swings in value? Of course there is much more to these businesses; however, why is there so much more to a company's stock price than the intrinsic value of the business? Many point to this type of stock market volatility to oppose the option of individual stock selection for private accounts. The use of a diversified collection of investments significantly reduces volatility.

Most of the more likely privatization program proposals would require the use of *lifestyle* portfolios built upon indexed (mutual) funds. Indexed funds invest in stocks, bonds, or other investment types on the basis of well known and published indexes. The goal is to mirror the performance of that index. The most common *stock* index is the S&P 500, which is made up of 500 of the largest public U.S. companies. Holdings are replaced in an index, periodically, to keep the index current. The more holdings that comprise an index the smaller should be the price volatility. Managed funds, on the other hand, rely on the expertise of the fund managers to buy and sell holdings as they see fit. The advantages of index funds are their low operating expenses, since there is very little trading activity and the expertise of fund managers is *not* required. A large disadvantage of using managed funds for Social Security private accounts would be the actual selection of the funds. Who would make the decisions as to which funds would be acceptable and how would we guard against any conflicts of interest? There have been studies comparing the long-term results of indexed vs. managed funds. I have read nothing objective and conclusive that one category is clearly better than the other. Some managed funds will perform better than comparable indexed funds and some will not.

Each *lifestyle* portfolio offered would be built upon an allocation of mutual funds. Indexed funds, where available, would most likely be used. One indexed fund might be comprised of short-term high quality notes which are considered very safe. However, they have no upside potential other than interest. Another fund could be an emerging market small stock fund with plenty of risk but with significant upside potential. There would be a range of funds in between these two extremes, with varying risk/return profiles. *Lifestyle* portfolios would be created based on these individual funds by using different percentage allocations of each. There would probably be 3 to 5 portfolios available with varying levels of overall risk. A portfolio more suitable for a younger worker would include more risky fund allocations to allow for greater growth potential. For someone nearest to retirement age it would include less risky fund allocations, with a resulting reduction in potential return. As a worker gets older, he or she should transition slowly from a more aggressive investment portfolio to one with less risk.

Other choices may be available, however, with the many legitimate concerns that have been raised regarding trust, risk and independence it is likely that the options will be very limited, at least initially.

It is interesting to take note of the fact that many of the strongest supporters of private accounts are fierce opponents of allowing the Trust Fund to hold investments other than government securities (in particular stocks). They believe that individuals should be allowed to have private account Social Security dollars invested in non government investments, but not the current Trust Fund. Their rationale is that the government should not be permitted ownership in private companies. Some economists believe that if the Social Security Trust Fund ceased to be considered a government asset, more diversified investments would be feasible, thus enhancing investment returns.

Will these accounts be made available for use prior to retirement? It is safe to assume that the private accounts will be available to beneficiaries upon the death of the wage earner and to the wage earner in the event of premature disability. Any use of the funds, prior to retirement age, obviously impacts the individual's retirement income. There has been some limited discussion of allowing use of funds in the case of extreme hardship or as a down payment for a first home.

How will the money be distributed out of the account upon retirement? Some proposals advocate requiring that the funds be used at retirement to purchase an annuity that provides lifetime income. Other proposals would limit the amount that could be withdrawn each year from the account, based on life expectancies. Other possibilities might include requiring distributions using one of the above options for a portion of the account, but no restrictions on the remainder of the account balance. Clearly, there is concern that there will be individuals who will not manage their private accounts effectively enough to safeguard their retirement income. The level of traditional Social Security benefits that an individual would be entitled to should also have an impact on the distribution flexibility available under the private accounts. The lure of a Ferrari, even at age 65, may be more than some retirees can resist.

How will benefits be taxed? It is assumed that there will continue to be income tax on a portion of benefit payments. Under private accounts, it is not clear where those taxes would be paid. It would most likely go into the Social Security Trust Fund to help cover liabilities for the traditional benefits. It is possible that the income taxes paid on the private account distributions could be credited to the Federal government as regular income taxes.

How will traditional benefits be impacted by the addition of private accounts? In exchange for the establishment of private accounts, there will be a reduction in the traditional benefits paid from the Trust Fund. However, just how will that reduction be determined? Here are three possibilities:

- Each wage earner would have a benefit determination based on only Social Security taxes paid to the *traditional* Trust Fund. These tax amounts would be accumulated to Social Security retirement age with investment credits. At retirement age, the Trust Fund would pay an annuity based upon this accumulated value.
- Each wage earner would receive a benefit from the Trust Fund that would reflect *all* contribu-

tions made into the program (including amounts paid into the private accounts) offset by the benefit that can be funded by the private account balance.

- Each wage earner would receive a benefit from the Trust Fund that would reflect only the wages for which taxes were paid to the *traditional* Trust Fund. This benefit amount would be based on a newly designed progressive benefit formula.

There are certainly many other approaches available.

What other changes would be part of a reform plan to add private accounts? The funded status of the current program is an issue that must be viewed in conjunction with any transition to private accounts. Some experts take the position that private accounts may reduce some of the unfunded liability by providing enhanced investment returns and possibly reducing some of the financial pressure on the traditional benefit obligations. If the goal were to eventually reach *permanent* solvency, the program would need to be transformed eventually to only private accounts. This of course would take generations to accomplish. In order to achieve this goal the $11.2 trillion unfunded liability previously described, would need to be fully satisfied. This can only be achieved through changes to the current program by a reduction in the traditional benefits or increases in Social Security taxes. In chapter 5, we discussed some of the possible changes that could be considered.

Will additional benefits be needed to supplement the private accounts? Social Security, as it exists today, is an insurance program designed to protect workers and their dependents. A pure individual account program will not have such a feature. It is true that in the early phases of any changes to a private account approach, the vast majority of benefits will still be the responsibility of the Trust Fund and not the private accounts. However, over time, a shift in emphasis will occur in favor of the private accounts. There will be workers who will become disabled or die before any meaningful benefits have accumulated in their private accounts. There will be seniors who will outlive their benefits due to unexpected longevity. There will be workers with low lifetime earnings who will count exclusively on Social Security benefits that may not be sufficient. Should there be some safety net built into the system or established under a separate program?

If you get the point that the implementation of private Social Security accounts are far more complicated than establishing an IRA or a 401k account, you get the picture. Many independent experts voice the opinion that these challenges should not be adequate reason to fully discount the consideration of some Social Security privatization.

Eight

RACHEL

I n the early days of Social Security, women had a significantly different place in the economic landscape of our
nation than they have today. Most women did not work outside
the home and were seldom significant breadwinners. They
were usually either married or widowed. Since they were
seldom the main income producers, insuring a loss of income
due to death, premature disability, or old age retirement was
not considered a priority. The focus of the Social Security
program was to regard them as dependents and beneficiaries.
In the past, women were much more likely to qualify for a
Social Security benefit based on 50% of the husband's benefit,
than a benefit based on their own wage histories.

Studies show that women rely more heavily on Social
Security to keep them out of poverty than do men. Men,
more often, have accumulated meaningful company
pension or 401k plan benefits. For this reason, many
women's groups have been at the forefront pushing for
changes to the Social Security program to improve its fiscal
solvency. Possible reductions in Social Security benefits due
to an inadequately financed program are of enormous
concern to many women. The majority of women and the
groups that represent their interests generally favor preserv-
ing the current Social Security program's overall structure
and improving its fiscal solvency. There are, however, certain
inadequacies that are of concern for which they hope

changes can be implemented.

There are some women's organizations that advocate not only the strengthening of the program but the addition of private accounts. They point to the significant increases in dual income households. In addition, there are more single working women, both with and without children. It is for these reasons that several organizations have expressed support of private Social Security accounts. Here are some reasons for this position:

- Many women today tend to move in and out of the workforce. They do this for the opportunity to spend more time with their children. Even when they are employed, they often hold part-time positions and often do not manage to earn meaningful pension or 401k benefits. Often, this category of worker will have fewer Social Security wages than is required to earn a benefit of at least 50% of their spouse's benefit. In some cases, they actually may have more wages and qualify for their own benefit, but the difference in benefit levels based on their wages and 50% of their husband's wages is small. Thus the taxes they paid into the program, in essence, yield no appreciable benefits. The use of privatized accounts would eliminate this phenomenon from occurring, since all amounts funded into private accounts would be available to provide benefits, based on the contributions paid into the private accounts.
- There are many single working women today with no eligible Social Security beneficiary. This is particularly troublesome in the case of women who work for many years and die prior

to retirement. Upon their death, there is no death benefit available. The use of privatized accounts would generate an asset that is inheritable and would therefore provide a death benefit to a loved one, charity or other organization of choice.

- There are many concerns with the current program that relate to our society's high rate of divorce. Most states provide that assets earned during a marriage are includable in determining each partner's share of property subject to division. Social Security benefits are not deemed assets and therefore do not come into consideration. The program does treat an ex-spouse as a beneficiary if the marriage lasted for at least 10 years. The average marriage that ends in divorce, however, lasts approximately 7 years. Private accounts that accumulated during marriage would be considered as assets of the marriage and subject to the division of property upon divorce, regardless of the length of marriage.

The above illustrate situations where the current program is disadvantageous to certain women, thus providing valid reasons to support private accounts. One area that merits some mention involves the differences in life expectancies between the sexes. The use of private accounts could have some unintended negative ramifications on women.

Under the current program, old age benefits are paid for the life of the retiree. Consider a male and a female with exactly the same wage history. They both elect to retire at age 65. Though the actual monthly benefit will be identical, the

value of the women's benefit is greater, since it is expected
to be paid for a longer time period. If one wished to purchase
a lifetime annuity from an insurance company the two principal individual factors used in determining the cost of the
annuity is the age and sex of the annuitant. At age 65, a
female could expect to pay approximately 10% more than
a male for the same lifetime monthly benefit. Therefore,
the current Social Security program subsidizes the benefits
for women at the cost of benefits for men, since men and
women pay the same tax rate. In the case of a married individual, this discrepancy is counterbalanced by the inclusion
of benefits for the spouse.

Let us turn to a private account program and do a similar
analysis. A man and a woman, both with identical wage histories, have made identical investments. They both retire at
age 65 and have the same account balances. They both
decide that they want to purchase annuities with their
accounts from an insurance company. The monthly benefit
the male will receive will be approximately 10% greater than
what his female counterpart will be entitled to. Let us assume
instead, that they do not wish to purchase the annuity but
instead elect to withdraw a fixed amount from their accounts
each month. Assuming that they withdraw the same monthly
benefit, it should last the same amount of time. It is very
unlikely, however, that *they* will last the same amount of time.
A 65-year-old female should live on average 3 to 4 years
longer than a 65-year-old male. Once again, in the case of a
married couple this is usually not an issue of significant
consequence for the reasons previously noted.

A movement to private accounts will not benefit all
women, even if we discount the life expectancy issue. Women
who never or seldom work outside the home and those in
families that are more traditional will continue to benefit
more from the *current* program. Single women with low life-

time wages who live to ripe old ages will also be better served under the current program. Since women still, on average, earn less than men do, the progressive nature of the current benefit formula is in their favor.

Once again, we have explored an area with valid arguments on each side of the debate. What is clear is that all women's groups are pushing for a strengthened Social Security system. Whether women collectively or individually are better off with the current program built around insurance or a private account system cannot be answered with any certainty.

Nine

ISHMAEL

I s the current Social Security program forsaking our
nation's minorities as Abraham neglected his son Ishmael?
Social Security came about at a time when the role of minorities in the nation's economy was not nearly as significant as
it is today. The program was primarily designed to meet the
needs of the white male population. Has it evolved enough
through the decades to be responsive to the concerns of our
nation's growing minorities?

Today we find that our country's minorities, in the same
way as women, are more dependent on Social Security than
is the white male population. It is estimated that 1/3 of all
African-American seniors rely on Social Security for their
entire retirement income. Without Social Security benefits,
the poverty rate for African-Americans would expect to
double. It is estimated that two thirds of Latinos' retirement
income is represented by Social Security benefits.
Consequently, the number one priority for our nation's
minority groups is the financial strengthening of the
program in order to assure that full benefits will continue to
be available.

Since the majority of our minority workers still tend to
earn less than the general population, it stands to reason
that they should fare better under the current program with
its progressive benefit structure than they would under a
privatized program. However, as is true with certain women's

groups, there are those representing the interests of minorities who not only support fiscal improvements to the program but also favor the idea of private accounts. The reasons for this position are as follows:

As previously explored, the current program is more valuable to those retirees with the longest longevity. Since many of our nation's minority groups experience shorter life expectancies, this tends to diminish the actual value of their benefits. Additionally, the general trend is for minorities to enter the workforce sooner and often pay into the system for more than 35 years. As discussed in Chapter 1, years in excess of 35 are not reflected in the determination of the Social Security benefit. Those who advocate the advantage of private accounts for our nation's minorities, claim that the combined effect of shorter life expectancies and earlier workforce entry often *mitigate* the progressive nature of the benefit structure.

Minorities are less likely to accumulate wealth during their lifetime due to lower income levels. Under a privatized Social Security program this would change due to the visibility of a tangible asset. The accumulation of assets often leads to psychological and social benefits that are important in the promoting of household welfare. This can also lead to increased opportunities for children.

There are several proposals that would consider allowing the use of private accounts, prior to retirement, as a down payment on a first home. The lack of funds for down payments is the leading reason that minorities continue to lag in the percentage of home ownership. The ownership of one's home, in addition to being an excellent investment, promotes the positive side effects that wealth accumulation produces.

There are many single working women of color in our society. As is the case for all women, the current program can be inequitable under certain circumstances. These situations include divorce prior to 10 years of marriage where the woman was not the primary breadwinner or upon death before retirement without an eligible Social Security beneficiary.

The position taken by the NAACP (National Association for the Advancement of Colored People) does not appear to support the privatization of Social Security. According to its President Dennis Hayes, "The assertion that Social Security is a bad deal for African–Americans, because our life expectancy is shorter than whites is misleading, because it assumes that blacks will forever die sooner than whites." Life expectancy rates are skewed as a result of the high mortality rate of young black males and that the difference in life expectancies at age 65 for black males compared to white males is only 2 years. In addition African-Americans between the ages of 50 and 59 are much more likely when compared with other workers in that age group to become disabled. As we noted, a pure private account program may not provide sufficient disability retirement benefits.

It should be apparent that the current program would continue to benefit some minority individuals and a privatized program would be more beneficial for others.

Ten

ABRAHAM AND JEREMIAH

T his chapter will focus on two final areas requiring explanation and exploration. The first will explain how our
nation managed to permit itself to accumulate such a large
level of unfunded liabilities under the current program. Is
it really because of errors in assumed mortality improvements, fertility rates, and the other assumptions used in the
calculation of the program's income and expenses? Or is
there more to it? The final area will be a brief exploration
of the prospects for change.

The key to understanding the future of our Social
Security program is in examining its past. As is often the
case, the road we go down is dictated by everything that has
come before. Had we not accumulated a *legacy debt* of the
current magnitude, it is unlikely that we would be involved
at all in this debate. I first encountered the term *legacy debt,*
while reading *Saving Social Security a Balanced Approach. Legacy
debt* represents all the accumulated expenses (benefits and
administrative) less all the accumulated income (payroll
taxes, income taxes and interest) on account of all prior and
current generations of Social Security retirees and beneficiaries. This also includes an adjustment to account for a
market rate of interest on the accumulating debt. The plain
indisputable truth is that those who have come before us
have, in general, done very well under the system. There
are certainly situations where individuals did not receive

from the program more benefits than the value of what was paid in on their behalf, but they are clearly in the minority. We can be proud of our generosity to those who came before us and helped to build the economy from which many of us have benefited. For those of us who do not share this sentiment, unfortunately, we cannot take the money back. Some seniors find the idea of a *legacy debt* confusing. They point to the Social Security Trust Fund surplus as proof that they actually contributed more to the program than they received in benefits. What they fail to recognize is the trillions of dollars contributed by the nearly 160 million citizens still working who have yet to receive a cent from the program. The current surplus, without the benefit of any future Social Security taxes, would only last about 3½ years. *Not much of a surplus if you look at it in those terms.*

In 1935, the concept of the program was to provide the initial retirees with benefits far more valuable than what they had paid into the system. It was not only humane, based on the problems of the time, but it also helped to relieve much of the burden on their families to support them in old age. This legacy of generosity was allowed to continue for a couple of reasons. No politician was inclined to cut benefits. The work force size, relative to the retiree size, could continue to support itself on a cash flow basis without an increase in taxes. Then in the early 1980s, it became clear that the party was ending. In 1983, changes were made to modify the normal retirement age and increase the tax rates. The idea was that retirees after the year 2000 should, in aggregate, pay more into the system in value than what they would get in benefits. The purpose of this was not only to prevent the *legacy debt* from increasing but, hopefully, to have it start to decrease. The assumptions that were used in those projections, as we have pointed out earlier, turned out to be optimistic and, therefore, we have not made much if any progress in paying down this *legacy debt*.

However, how important is it to pay this debt down? Think of it as a loan that you took out and *gave* to your parents. Let us assume that the institution you borrowed the funds from only requires that you pay back the interest and not the principal. As long as you believe that you will continue to be able to afford to pay the interest, it is not critical that you pay off the principal. Now you pass away and your children inherit this loan. They have the same obligation to either pay off the loan principal or continue to pay the loan interest. Let us assume that they also just pay the interest and pass the loan principal debt on to your grandchildren. This can continue theoretically in perpetuity. At what point is it appropriate for one generation to no longer pass the loan along to the next generation? If Abraham had gotten Social Security benefits would you want to keep paying for them today?

Now, let us address the question of where we might be heading. The President has embraced the Social Security reform issue as being an important piece of his legacy. The precise motivation for his zeal, only he knows for sure, although it appears that his desire to see a transformation to private accounts is the driving force. He could otherwise have focused on proposals that would maintain the current program design but strengthen it, fiscally, by the use of benefit reductions and tax increases. It is likely that he perceives that the current program is unfair, even though it would be possible to remove some of these inequities from the program without so radical a move as the push for privatization. He may believe that privatization is the only road to a permanent solution for fiscal solvency that theoretically could come generations later, when all taxes and benefits would run through private accounts.

As of this writing, many congressional Republicans have

been slow at endorsing the President's push for private accounts with any great fervor. Some of those who are enthusiastic supporters of private accounts have floated their own proposals. There are at least a half dozen of them so far, and probably many more to come. There are many differences in these proposals, ranging from modest private account contribution rates with highly restricted investment options to high private account contribution rates and very flexible investment options. Those Republicans, who have not yet formally embraced private accounts, do generally embrace reform to improve the program's long-term solvency. Many Republican members of Congress represent districts where constituents are very wary of the idea of private accounts. These members of Congress are concerned that by embracing private accounts this position could backfire in the 2006 congressional races. They are anxiously waiting to see how well the President does with his sales pitch to the American people before committing publicly. It is fair to say that if the President feels he is getting the job done there will be some serious arm-twisting in Washington, later this year.

Where do the Democratic lawmakers stand on the issue? Needless to say, if the President and the Republicans say it is good, then *they* must claim it is bad. Nevertheless, there are two different camps in the Democratic aisles. There are those Democrats who, like the Republicans, believe that it is important to take action in the not too distant future to shore up the program, financially. Then there are those who take the position that there is neither a crisis nor any need to rush into change. Their position is that this "crisis" has been politically created so that the President can sell his private account proposal. There are, as of the writing of this book, no Democrats who are outwardly lining up to support private accounts, but there are most probably, some behind-the-scene discussions taking place by some of the more open-minded Congressional members.

Federal Reserve Chairman Alan Greenspan, one of the key players in the 1983 Social Security overhaul, has provided an endorsement for private accounts, but not without some cautionary comments. He applauds the idea of the potential ability to create a sense of increased wealth on the part of middle and lower income workers. However, he expresses concern that increased government debt, which would be needed to bring the accounts to fruition, would boost several key interest rates affecting a broad range of consumer borrowing.

Special interest groups have been weighing in with positions that support the best interests of their members. Objectivity is not their mission. They make themselves heard by using the media and, of course, by *sharing* their positions with members of Congress. Two organizations, in particular, who have made their voices clear, are AARP (which needs no introduction) and NAM, the National Association of Manufacturers, which represents about 14,000 companies. These two organizations are on opposite sides of the Social Security debate. I believe a look at a couple of articles that I found on their respective websites gives us an idea of how easy it is to reach different conclusions on the same topic.

AARP: Myths and Truths about Social Security

Quote 1: "So, is Social Security going to go bust? Not by a long shot. In fact, Social Security is in better shape today that at any other time since it was enacted in 1935. That is because of some judicious adjustments suggested in 1983 by a commission set up by Ronald Reagan and headed by Alan Greenspan. Since then, trust fund reserves have gone up from nearly zero to $1.6 trillion."

Comment: Trust fund reserves have, in fact, gone up from nearly zero to $1.6 trillion. However the statement that because there are greater reserves now than ever before, the program is in better shape, can be misleading. If one had liabilities of $3,000 and reserves (assets) of $1,000, would that be better than liabilities of $1,500 and reserves of zero? To judge fiscal solvency on the basis of assets (reserves) without considering the level of liabilities is an incomplete analysis. In 1983, after the reforms were made, the program was projected to have enough income to pay all benefits for 75 years, on a cash flow basis. According to the Social Security actuaries, the program can now make that claim for only 37 years. How exactly is that "in better shape"?

Quote 2: "from 2018 through 2027, incoming tax revenues combined with interest earnings will still be enough to pay benefits and build the trust fund balance."

Comment: This is an accurate statement; however, there is no mention of where the interest earnings are to come from. It is due from the Federal Treasury, as explained in Chapter 2. This will most likely necessitate income tax increases, reduction in government spending, or borrowing from other sources. The amount of the annual interest that will be needed in 2020 is estimated to be $85 billion and by 2025 is estimated to be approximately $281 billion.

NAM: To the Point: Social Security Reform

Quote 1: "To pay benefits to future retirees without reform, we'd have to increase FICA taxes by nearly 70 percent (from 10.5 to 17.7 percent)."

Comment: This statement omits when such an increase would become effective. According to the 2004 Social Security report an immediate increase of 1.9%, from 12.4% to 14.3% would bring the program into 75-year cash flow solvency.

Quote 2: "Private retirement accounts would likely yield retirement savings much greater than the average 2 % annual Social Security return."

Comment: This 2% number is often used as a tool to make us believe that our taxes are being invested in a fund comparable to a money market account earning only 2% interest. The Trust Fund is currently earning approximately 6% interest. The 2% number is not the return on the Trust fund; it is some measure of the expected average return on payroll taxes when we factor in the cost of the *legacy debt*. This debt will continue to exist whether or not we move toward private accounts.

I have only used AARP and NAM as examples. They are not alone in their crusades to gain support from the public and Congress. This is how many special interest groups operate. We will not change this system, no matter how hard we try. In many cases, these organizations do very important work for their members. We must be diligent in our analysis when reviewing positions taken by such organizations.

As of this writing, there is so much polarization on the Social Security issue; it is difficult to believe that anything can be accomplished, unless there are dramatic shifts in sentiment. There are, as previously discussed, two primary approaches being discussed to strengthen the current program and reform through the use of private accounts. It does not appear, at least at this point, that the President would be interested in just modifying the program to shore it up fiscally, without private accounts as part of the package. Those Republicans who have yet to commit to private accounts would need to hear from their constituents that supporting private accounts would not hurt them politically. If that happens, the Republicans do have the votes to push reform into law, if they can agree on the specifics. Nevertheless, without more than token support from the Democrats, they may not wish to do so. In order to get such support they would have to give something in return. What would that be? Your guess is as good as mine.

Before we move on, I want to share a prophecy. I do not believe that Jeremiah is responsible for this one, nor do I necessarily think it will come to pass. However, it is interesting to ponder.

We are in the early 2020s (no meteor has solved our funding problem) and, as projected, the Social Security taxes have exceeded the benefit payouts through 2017. Unfortunately, the country has been so polarized on what changes were appropriate that no action has been taken. The Federal government has not been at all responsible with balancing the budget and has continued to use the Trust Fund surpluses in addition to other borrowing. The national debt now exceeds $20 trillion. The Federal government started to repay the Trust Fund in 2018 as needed to make benefit payments.

The initial year's repayment will be modest but by 2025 it will reach $281 billion just for that year. Those in control in 2005, the baby boomers who did not push our Legislators to act today, will be retired and receiving their Social Security checks (direct deposit, of course). Many of them will depend on their Social Security benefits to maintain the standard of living they planned for in retirement. Today's taxpayers, currently in their twenties and thirties, will be running the country in 2025. There is an enormous national debt and strong global economy where the U.S. dollar is no longer king, making borrowing very expensive. These new leaders are aware that we faced this issue in 2005 and were unable and unwilling to act, thus putting this financial burden on them. If you do not think that cutting Social Security benefits for retirees could be one of the solutions, then think again.

CONCLUSION

Congratulations for making it through. I hope that this book has managed to convey just how complicated the issue of Social Security reform actually is. Too often, we are swayed to positions that we would not embrace if we understood more of the implications associated with that position. In a democracy, change is appropriate when the majority feel it is in the public's best interest. This is true even though changes in the law will affect different groups of citizens, differently, some positive and others negative. We need to make sure we truly understand these effects before we decide to act or elect to continue the status quo.

We often feel that our opinions have little effect on how our congressional members represent us. Social Security reform is one of those few situations where they truly want to know where we stand. Some of them may be motivated by their own self-interests. There is the fear of making a mistake that could endanger their political careers. Others want to know our opinions, in recognition of the importance and complexity of the problem to be addressed. We must use their fear and concern to encourage them to work together, to come up with a solution that embraces the values that we, Americans, hold dear, compassion, equality, and responsibility.

The Social Security reform debate is filled with economic, political, social, and philosophical issues. The economic issues often come down to sophisticated number crunching. This helps us to recognize to what extent a financial problem exists and, if there is one requiring change, whether a proposed solution will be effective. The political issues are driven by what our leaders perceive will be the most accept-able course of action in the eyes of the public. There are always multiple avenues that our elected leaders can follow but what they consider likely to keep them in office is the position that will usually win their support. The social issues reflect the fact that we live in a pluralistic society, where it is impossible to develop a single program that will be compat-ible with the specific goals and challenges of different demo-graphic groups. These goals and challenges are not static; they change with time, as does the nation's demographics and their degree of influence on key issues. Back in the 1940s, there were very few retirees relative to workers. Minorities and women were a much smaller piece of the economic picture. This has all changed. The philosophical issues come about as we ponder the *role* of government. Should the government force a retirement system on us? How flexible should it be? What social purpose should it advance, if any? Moreover, if there is no program in place, how do we treat those who will not be able to support them-selves in old age, or in the event of unexpected misfortune? Are social safety nets a crutch that causes individuals to do less and expect more from society? These questions should be answered as part of a national debate on Social Security reform.

Our founding fathers were, for the most part, of the opinion that government should be small. Remember, that it was an unfair tax that was the catalyst for the Revolutionary War. Not until the New Deal, did big government become a way of life, providing a vast majority of our population with a standard of living that they may never have experienced. The pendulum is now swinging the other way, back to the idea of less government involvement in social programs. It is the belief of some that people will accomplish more when they have less guaranteed, and that families, communities, religious organizations and charities will assist those truly in need. It is an idea that is centuries old, but does it work?

I attended a conference at the Cato institute in Washington D.C. titled *Social Security, the Opportunity for Real Reform*. Cato is a non-profit, tax exempt, educational foundation serving to advance public policy positions that limit the role of government in the lives of its citizens. The conference featured many well-respected experts in the field of Social Security reform, as well as members of Congress and representatives from the Social Security Administration. Cato is an organization that has advanced many popular ideas and has been at the forefront of the Social Security debate for over 20 years. It is clear in its goal to reform Social Security to include privatized accounts. At the conference, I met a young woman who was diligently taking copious notes. I asked her what her interest was in attending this conference. She responded that she was a concerned citizen looking for clarification of the relevant issues and proposed solutions to the funding crisis. She felt utterly confused by the media coverage of the debate, and felt that she needed to go to the *source* for factual information. I asked her if she had heard any speakers at the conference who put forth proposals that seriously entertained a solution that did *not* include private accounts or totally dismantling the system. Her response was that she had not, but she believed that if she could not get the straight story in Washington, D.C., then where else could she get it. I then asked her *which* straight story was she after.

Friends, family and professional associates who are aware of my passion on this subject enjoy engaging me in conversation about Social Security issues. I am only too happy to oblige them. When they ask if I think the program should continue without change, my answer is that all programs need change periodically, and Social Security is due for one. When they ask me whether private accounts are a good idea, I answer, "Read my book." When they ask me for my thoughts on the ideal (if possible) government sponsored Social Security program, I respond with the following comments:

To dismantle our Social Security program that has been around so long and worked so well is foolish and unfair to those who have been depending on it for a secure retirement. *This does not mean, however, that it should not be evolving.* Below are the principles that I support that should be the guide to redesigning Social Security

- The overwhelming majority of the public should consider the program as reasonably fair. Any provisions that exist that might undermine that sentiment should be reviewed for possible modification.
- There are hard working citizens who will require or desire fixed life time benefits from the program in the case of premature disability, death, or in their old age. The program should protect and accommodate them.
- The *legacy debt* must be addressed in a serious way. We must recognize our responsibility to future generations and act on it now.
- The Federal government must stop being dependent on Social Security surpluses. We must start providing for annual balanced Federal budgets, without reliance on Social Security funds.
- There are individuals with lifestyles that were not considered when the program was developed. The program must be modified to meet their needs.

You should have noticed that private accounts were not mentioned in the above. If you have deducted that I am not in favor of them then you are wrong. If you have concluded that I am in favor of them, you are also wrong. I have no objection or passion for them. If they are used properly they could be advantageous to the program and if not, they could create new problems. However, I do not believe they should be the driving force in any program reform that we are considering today.

I have found that the most vocal constituents on this issue are senior citizens, the ones that are the least likely to be impacted by any changes. Seniors also tend to be the group that is less likely to encourage any meaningful reform. There are no proposals that I am aware of that would negatively impact benefits for current retirees or near term retirees. If there were, it would never see the light of day. This country needs our *younger and middle aged* citizens to take control of the debate in an open and creative manner.

We need to encourage our elected officials to find some common ground on the relevant issues, and then build on them, as opposed to using the program as a lightning rod for political gamesmanship. Obviously, my conclusions represent my point of view. Now, it is time for your opinion. Don't let biased media, special interest groups, or some narrow-minded politicians make it for you.

APPENDIX

For those readers who find that tables are helpful, I have included several in this Appendix.

Table 1: Worker to Retiree Ratios

Table 2:   Life Expectancies at Age 65

Table 3: Annual Trust Fund Cash Flow

Table 4: $100 Then Is Worth How Much Today?

Table 5: Wage Bases, Tax Rates & Maximum Contributions

Tables 1-3 and 5 are based on data from the Social Security administration 2004 report. Data after 2003 is on a projected basis using the intermediate set of assumptions.

Table 4 is based on the U.S. Department of Labor; Bureau of Labor Statistics; Consumer Price Index for Urban Consumers.

TABLE 1: WORKER TO RETIREE RATIOS

	HISTORIC		**PROJECTED**
YEAR	**WORKERS PER RETIREE**	**YEAR**	**WORKERS PER RETIREE**
1945	41.9	2005	3.3
1950	16.5	2010	3.2
1955	8.6	2015	2.9
1960	5.1	2020	2.6
1965	4.0	2025	2.3
1970	3.7	2030	2.2
1975	3.2	2035	2.1
1980	3.2	2040	2.0
1985	3.3	2045	2.0
1990	3.4	2050	2.0
1991	3.3	2055	2.0
1992	3.3	2060	2.0
1993	3.3	2065	1.9
1994	3.3	2070	1.9
1995	3.3	2075	1.9
1996	3.3	2080	1.9
1997	3.3		
1998	3.4		
1999	3.4		
2000	3.4		
2001	3.4		
2002	3.3		
2003	3.3		

Retiree includes old age pensioners, disability retirees, and beneficiaries

TABLE 2: LIFE EXPECTANCIES AT AGE 65

HISTORIC   ### PROJECTED

YEAR	MALE	FEMALE	YEAR	MALE	FEMALE
1940	11.9	13.4	2005	16.1	19.0
1945	12.6	14.4	2010	16.4	19.1
1950	12.8	15.1	2015	16.7	19.4
1955	13.1	15.6	2020	17.1	19.7
1960	12.9	15.9	2025	17.4	20.0
1965	12.9	16.3	2030	17.7	20.3
1970	13.1	17.1	2035	18.0	20.6
1975	13.7	18.0	2040	18.2	20.9
1980	14.0	18.4	2045	18.5	21.2
1985	14.4	18.6	2050	18.8	21.4
1990	15.0	19.0	2055	19.1	21.7
1991	15.1	19.1	2060	19.3	22.0
1992	15.2	19.2	2065	19.6	22.2
1993	15.1	19.0	2070	19.9	22.5
1994	15.3	19.0	2075	20.1	22.7
1995	15.3	19.0	2080	20.3	22.9
1996	15.4	19.0			
1997	15.5	19.1			
1998	15.6	19.0			
1999	15.7	18.9			
2000	15.8	18.9			
2001	15.9	18.9			
2002	16.0	18.9			
2003	16.0	19.0			

TABLE 3: ANNUAL TRUST FUND CASH FLOW

Year	Taxes	Interest	Expenses	Balance
2004	565	89	500	1,684
2005	605	96	518	1,867
2006	635	104	538	2,068
2007	667	115	563	2,287
2008	702	129	594	2,524
2009	735	143	632	2,770
2010	772	158	670	3,030
2011	812	173	712	3,303
2012	851	190	760	3,584
2013	889	206	812	3,867
2015	973	242	927	4,442
2020	1,214	325	1,299	5,776
2025	1,501	375	1,782	6,575
2030	1,852	371	2,364	6,370
2035	2,285	287	3,032	4,736
2040	2,818	101	3,778	1,280

Amounts in Billions of Dollars

Trust Fund balance as of the beginning of 2004 was $1,531 Billion.

Taxes represent Social Security taxes and income tax on Social Security benefits.

Interest is the interest earned on the U.S. Government securities held by the Trust Fund.

Expenses are the sum of benefits paid and administrative expenses.

Balance is the accumulated Trust Fund surplus at the end of the year.

The above represents the total of the Old Age, Survivor and Disability Trust Funds

TABLE 4: $ 100 Then Is Worth How Much Today

Year	2004 Value	Year	2004 Value	Year	2004 Value
1945	$ 1,049	1965	$ 600	1985	$ 176
1946	$ 969	1966	$ 583	1986	$ 172
1947	$ 847	1967	$ 566	1987	$ 166
1948	$ 784	1968	$ 543	1988	$ 160
1949	$ 794	1969	$ 515	1989	$ 152
1950	$ 784	1970	$ 487	1990	$ 145
1951	$ 727	1971	$ 466	1991	$ 139
1952	$ 713	1972	$ 452	1992	$ 135
1953	$ 708	1973	$ 426	1993	$ 131
1954	$ 702	1974	$ 383	1994	$ 127
1955	$ 705	1975	$ 351	1995	$ 124
1956	$ 694	1976	$ 332	1996	$ 120
1957	$ 672	1977	$ 312	1997	$ 118
1958	$ 654	1978	$ 290	1998	$ 116
1959	$ 649	1979	$ 260	1999	$ 113
1960	$ 638	1980	$ 229	2000	$ 110
1961	$ 632	1981	$ 208	2001	$ 107
1962	$ 625	1982	$ 196	2002	$ 105
1963	$ 617	1983	$ 190	2003	$ 103
1964	$ 609	1984	$ 182	2004	$ 100

Example: $100 in 1954 had the same approximate purchasing power as $702 in 2004.

TABLE 5: WAGE BASES, TAX RATES,
& MAXIMUM CONTRIBUTIONS

Year	Base	Rate	Maximum	Year	Base	Rate	Maximum
1937-49	$ 3,000	2.000	$ 60.00	1981	$ 29,700	10.700	$ 3,177.90
1950	$ 3,000	3.000	$ 90.00	1982	$ 32,400	10.800	$ 3,499.20
1951-53	$ 3,600	3.000	$ 108.00	1983	$ 35,700	10.800	$ 3,855.60
1954	$ 3,600	4.000	$ 144.00	1984	$ 37,800	11.400	$ 4,309.20
1955-56	$ 4,200	4.000	$ 168.00	1985	$ 39,600	11.400	$ 4,514.40
1957-58	$ 4,200	4.500	$ 189.00	1986	$ 42,000	11.400	$ 4,788.00
1959	$ 4,800	5.000	$ 240.00	1987	$ 43,800	11.400	$ 4,993.20
1960-61	$ 4,800	6.000	$ 288.00	1988	$ 45,000	12.120	$ 5,454.00
1962	$ 4,800	6.250	$ 300.00	1989	$ 48,000	12.120	$ 5,817.60
1963-65	$ 4,800	7.250	$ 348.00	1990	$ 51,300	12.400	$ 6,361.20
1966	$ 6,600	7.700	$ 508.20	1991	$ 53,400	12.400	$ 6,621.60
1967	$ 6,600	7.800	$ 514.80	1992	$ 55,500	12.400	$ 6,882.00
1968	$ 7,800	7.600	$ 592.80	1993	$ 57,600	12.400	$ 7,142.40
1969	$ 7,800	8.400	$ 655.20	1994	$ 60,600	12.400	$ 7,514.40
1970	$ 7,800	8.400	$ 655.20	1995	$ 61,200	12.400	$ 7,588.80
1971	$ 7,800	9.200	$ 717.60	1996	$ 62,700	12.400	$ 7,774.80
1972	$ 9,000	9.200	$ 828.00	1997	$ 65,400	12.400	$ 8,109.60
1973	$ 10,800	9.700	$ 1,047.60	1998	$ 68,400	12.400	$ 8,481.60
1974	$ 13,200	9.900	$ 1,306.80	1999	$ 72,600	12.400	$ 9,002.40
1975	$ 14,100	9.900	$ 1,395.90	2000	$ 76,200	12.400	$ 9,448.80
1976	$ 15,300	9.900	$ 1,514.70	2001	$ 80,400	12.400	$ 9,969.60
1977	$ 16,500	9.900	$ 1,633.50	2002	$ 84,900	12.400	$ 10,527.60
1978	$ 17,700	10.100	$ 1,787.70	2003	$ 87,000	12.400	$ 10,788.00
1979	$ 22,900	10.160	$ 2,326.64	2004	$ 87,900	12.400	$ 10,899.60
1980	$ 25,900	10.160	$ 2,631.44	2005	$ 90,000	12.400	$ 11,160.00

REFERENCES

1. The Bible (not really)
2. The Complete Idiot's Guide to Social Security; (oops) by Lita Epstein
3. Saving Social Security A Balanced Approach; by Peter A. Diamond and Peter R. Orszag
4. Pension Planning (9th Edition); by Everett T. Allen Jr., Joseph J. Melone, Jerry S. Rosenbloom and Dennis F. Mahoney
5. The 2004 Annual Report of the Board of Trustees of the Federal Old-Age and Survivors Insurance and Disability Insurance Trust Funds.
6. Common Objections to a Market-Based Social Security System: a Response; by Melissa Hieger and William Shipman
7. www.naacp.org/news/2005/2005-02-03.html
8. www.aarpmagazine.org/money/Articles/myths_ and_ truths_about_social_security.html
9. www.nam.org/s_nam/doc1.asp?cid=201961 &did=202064
10. www.hesstonrecord.com/web/isite.dll?1081217172734
11. www.brillig.com/debt_clock
12. www.socialsecurity.org/daily/09-29-00.html
13. ftp.bls.gov/pub/special.requests/cpi/cpiai.txt

ABOUT THE AUTHOR

Mark Shemtob is the President of an independent pension consulting firm located in Morris County, New Jersey. During the last 25 years he has worked with a variety of employers providing comprehensive services in the design, administration and analysis of all categories of retirement programs. Mark is an Enrolled Actuary under ERISA, an associate of the Society of Actuaries, a member of the American Academy of Actuaries and a member of the American Society of Pension Professionals and Actuaries.

He has written for the New Jersey CPA magazine on pension topics of interest and teaches at Rutgers University on the various aspects of our country's individual, business and government retirement programs. Mark received his B.S. from SUNY at Albany and his M.A. from Columbia University both degrees in mathematics.

Mark resides in Mendham, New Jersey with his wife Jane and two sons Zach and Jason. He can be reached by email at markeaasa@yahoo.com.